BIOG TEEGE TEE
My grandfather would have
shot me : a black woman
discovers her family's Nazi
past
Teege, Jennifer, 1970-

D0015795

MY GRANDFATHER
WOULD HAVE SHOT ME

THE EXPERIMENT

BECAUSE EVERY BOOK IS A TEST OF NEW IDEAS

MY GRANDFATHER
WOULD HAVE SHOT ME

A BLACK WOMAN DISCOVERS
HER FAMILY'S NAZI PAST

JENNIFER TEEGE
AND NIKOLA SELLMAIR

TRANSLATED BY CAROLIN SOMMER

THE EXPERIMENT

NEW YORK

MY GRANDFATHER WOULD HAVE SHOT ME: *A Black Woman Discovers Her Family's Nazi Past*

Originally published under the title *Amon: Mein Grossvater hätte mich erschossen*
Copyright © 2013, 2015 by Rowohlt Verlag GmbH, Reinbek bei Hamburg;
Copyright © 2013, 2015 by Jennifer Teege and Nikola Sellmair
Translation copyright © 2015 by Carolin Sommer
The translation of this work was supported by a grant from the Goethe-Institut
which is funded by the German Ministry of Foreign Affairs.

All photographs are courtesy of the author or in the public domain,
except for the following, which are used with permission:
ullstein bild, Berlin: 8 (AP), 57 (imagebroker.net/Petr Svarc)
Nikola Sellmair/stern/Picture Press, Hamburg: 45
Sueddeutsche Zeitung Photo, Munich: 28 (Teutopress)
Yad Vashem Photo Archive, Jerusalem: 33, 39, 51, 53, 63, 91 (Emil Dobel)
Diane Vincent, Berlin: 194, 196

All rights reserved. Except for brief passages quoted in newspaper, magazine, radio, television, or online reviews, no portion of this book may be reproduced, distributed, or transmitted in any form or by any means, electronic or mechanical, including photocopying, recording, or information storage or retrieval system, without the prior written permission of the publisher.

Some of the names of people, and identifying details, have been changed to protect the privacy of individuals.

Many of the designations used by manufacturers and sellers to distinguish their products are claimed as trademarks. Where those designations appear in this book and The Experiment was aware of a trademark claim, the designations have been capitalized.

The Experiment, LLC
220 East 23rd Street, Suite 301
New York, NY 10010-4674
www.theexperimentpublishing.com

The Experiment's books are available at special discounts when purchased in bulk for premiums and sales promotions as well as for fund-raising or educational use. For details, contact us at info@theexperimentpublishing.com.

Library of Congress Cataloging-in-Publication Data

Teege, Jennifer, 1970-
[Amon. English]
My grandfather would have shot me : a Black woman discovers her family's Nazi past / Jennifer Teege, Nikola Sellmair.
    pages cm
"Originally published under the title Amon : mein Grossvater hätte mich erschossen"--Title page verso.
Includes bibliographical references.
ISBN 978-1-61519-253-3 (cloth) — ISBN 978-1-61519-254-0 (ebook)
1. Teege, Jennifer, 1970- 2. Teege, Jennifer, 1970---Family. 3. Grandchildren of war criminals—Germany—Biography. 4. Racially mixed people—Germany—Biography. 5. Göth, Amon, 1908-1946--Family. 6. Nazis—Family relationships. 7. Concentration camp commandants—Family relationships. 8. Plaszów (Concentration camp) 9. Teege, Jennifer, 1970—Travel—Poland. 10. Teege, Jennifer, 1970—Homes and haunts—Israel. I. Sellmair, Nikola, 1971- II. Title.
    CT1098.T33A3 2015
    929.20943—dc23
                                        2014046242

Cover design by Christopher Brian King
Cover and author photographs by Thorsten Wulff

Text design by Pauline Neuwirth, Neuwirth & Associates, Inc.

Manufactured in the United States of America
Distributed by Workman Publishing Company, Inc.
Distributed simultaneously in Canada by Thomas Allen & Son Ltd.

First printing April 2015
10 9 8 7 6 5 4 3 2 1

FOR Y.

CONTENTS

MY GRANDFATHER
WOULD HAVE SHOT ME

THE DISCOVERY

T IS THE LOOK on the woman's face that seems familiar. I'm standing in the central library in Hamburg, and in my hands I'm holding a red book that I've just picked up from the shelf. The spine reads: *I Have to Love My Father, Don't I?* On the front cover is a small black-and-white photograph of a middle-aged woman. She looks deep in thought, and there is something strained and joyless about her. The corners of her mouth are turned down; she looks unhappy.

I glance quickly at the subtitle: *The Life Story of Monika Goeth, Daughter of the Concentration Camp Commandant from "Schindler's List."* Monika Goeth! I know that name; it's my mother's name. My mother, who put me in an orphanage when I was little and whom I haven't seen in many years.

I was also called Goeth once. I was born with that name, wrote "Jennifer Goeth" on my first schoolbooks. It was my name until after I was adopted, when I took on the surname of my adoptive parents. I was seven years old.

Why is my mother's name on this book? I am staring at the cover. In the background, behind the black-and-white photo of the woman, is a shadowy picture of a man with his mouth open and a rifle in his hands. That must be the concentration camp commandant.

I open the book and start leafing through its pages, slowly at first, then faster and faster. It contains not only text but lots of photos, too. The people in the pictures—haven't I seen them somewhere before? One is a tall, young woman with dark hair; she reminds me of my mother. Another is an older woman in a flowery summer dress, sitting in the English Garden in Munich. I don't have many pictures of my grandmother, but I know each of them very well. In one of them she is wearing the exact same dress as this woman. The caption under the photo says *Ruth Irene Goeth*. That was my grandmother's name.

Is this my family? Are these pictures of my mother and my grandmother? Surely not, that would be absurd: It can't be that there is a book about my family and I know nothing about it!

I quickly skim through the rest of the book. Right at the back, on the last page, I find a biography, and it begins like this: "Monika Goeth, born in Bad Toelz in 1945." I know these dates; they are on my adoption papers. And here they are, in black and white. It really is my mother. This book *is* about my family.

I snap the book shut. It is quiet. Somewhere in the reading room someone is coughing. I need to get out of here, quickly; I need to be alone with this book. Clutching it close to me like a precious treasure, I just barely manage to walk down the stairs and through the checkout. I don't take in the librarian's face as she hands the book back to me. I walk out onto the expansive square in front of the library. My knees buckle. I lie down on a bench and close my eyes. Traffic rushes past me.

My car is parked nearby, but I can't drive now. A couple of times I sit up and consider reading on, but I am dreading it. I want to read the book at home, in peace and quiet, cover to cover.

It is a warm, sunny August day, but my hands are as cold as ice. I call my husband. "You have to come and get me; I have found a book. About my mother and my family."

Why did my mother never tell me? Do I mean that little to her, still? Who is this Amon Goeth? What exactly did he do? Why do I know nothing about him? What was the story of *Schindler's List* again? And what about the people I've heard referred to as Schindler Jews?

It has been a long time since I've seen the film. I remember that it came out in the middle of the 1990s, while I was studying in Israel. Everybody was talking about Steven Spielberg's Holocaust movie. I didn't watch it until later, on Israeli TV, alone in my room in my shared flat, in Rehov Engel—Engel Street—in Tel Aviv. I recall that I was touched by the film, but that I thought the end was a bit kitschy, too Hollywood.

Schindler's List was just a film to me; it didn't have anything to do with me personally.

Why has nobody told me the truth? Has everybody been lying to me for all these years?

CHAPTER 1

ME, GRANDDAUGHTER OF A
MASS MURDERER

In Germany, the Holocaust is family history.

—RAUL HILBERG

WAS BORN ON JUNE 29, 1970, the daughter of Monika Goeth
and a Nigerian father. When I was four weeks old, my mother
took me to a Catholic orphanage and put me in the care of the
nuns.

At three, I was taken in by a foster family, who then adopted me
when I was seven. My skin is black, while that of my adoptive
parents and two brothers is white. Everybody could see that I was
not their biological child, but my adoptive parents always reassured me that they loved me just as much as their own children.
They took me and my brothers to playgroups and Gymboree
classes. As a child, I still saw my biological mother and grandmother, but we lost contact as I grew older. I was 21 when I last
saw my mother.

Then, at age 38, I found *the book*. Why on earth did I pick it up
off the shelf, one among hundreds of thousands of books? Is there
such a thing as fate?

The day had begun just as usual. My husband had gone to work;
I had taken my sons to preschool and then gone into town to visit
the library. I go there often. I like the concentrated silence, the

quiet footsteps, the rustling noise of turning pages, the reading visitors hunched over their books. I was looking for something about depression in the psychology department. There, at hip level, between Erich Fromm's *The Art of Loving* and a book with the vague title *The Power Lies in the Crisis,* was the book with the red cover. I had never heard of the author, Matthias Kessler, but the title sounded interesting: *I Have to Love My Father, Don't I?* So I took the book from the shelf.

When my husband Goetz comes to pick me up, he finds me lying on the bench in front of the library. He sits down beside me, examines the book, and starts leafing through its pages. I snatch it back from him. I don't want him to read it first because I've realized that the book is meant for me, the key to my family history, to my life. The key I've been looking for all these years.

For my whole life I had felt that there was something wrong with me: behind my sadness, my depression. But I could never quite put my finger on what was so fundamentally wrong.

Goetz takes my hand and we walk over to his car. I hardly say a word on the way home. He takes the rest of the day off and looks after our two sons.

I collapse onto our bed and read and read, to the very last page. It is dark when I close the book. Then I sit down at my computer and spend the whole night online, reading everything I can find about Amon Goeth. I feel like I have entered a chamber of horrors. I read about his decimation of the Polish ghettoes, his sadistic murders, the dogs he trained to tear humans apart. It is only now that I realize the magnitude of the crimes Amon Goeth committed. Himmler, Goebbels, Goering—I know who they are. But what exactly Amon Goeth had done, I'd had no idea. Slowly I begin to grasp that the Amon Goeth in the film *Schindler's List* is not a fictional character, but a person who actually existed in flesh and blood. A man who killed people by the dozens and, what is more, who enjoyed it. My grandfather. I am the granddaughter of a mass murderer.

■　　■　　■

Jennifer Teege has a deep, warm voice with a hint of a Munich accent, slightly rolling her "R"s. Her face is bright, she doesn't wear make-up; her naturally frizzy hair is tamed into long black curls. Tight fitted pants hug her long, thin legs. When she enters a room she turns heads, and men's eyes follow her around. She walks upright, with a firm, determined step.

Her friends describe Jennifer as a confident woman, inquisitive and full of adventure. A college friend says, "If she heard about an exciting country, she'd say, 'I've not been there, I'll go and visit!' And off she'd go—to Egypt, Laos, Vietnam, and Mozambique."

But when she talks about her family history, her hands tremble and she begins to cry.

The moment when Jennifer found the book with the library code Mcm O GOET#KESS is the moment that cut her life in two, into a before and an after: A *before*, when she lived without knowledge of her family's past, and an *after*, living with that knowledge.

The whole world knows her grandfather's story: In Steven Spielberg's film *Schindler's List*, the cruel concentration camp commandant Amon Goeth is Oskar Schindler's drinking buddy and adversary: Two men born in the same year, one a murderer of Jews, the other their savior. One particular scene has stuck in the collective memory: Amon Goeth shooting prisoners from his balcony, his personal form of morning exercise.

As commandant of the Płaszów concentration camp, Amon Goeth was responsible for the deaths of thousands of people. In 1946, he was hanged in Krakow; his ashes were thrown in the Vistula River. Goeth's lover Ruth Irene, Jennifer Teege's beloved grandmother, denied his crimes ever after. In 1983 she killed herself with an overdose of sleeping pills.

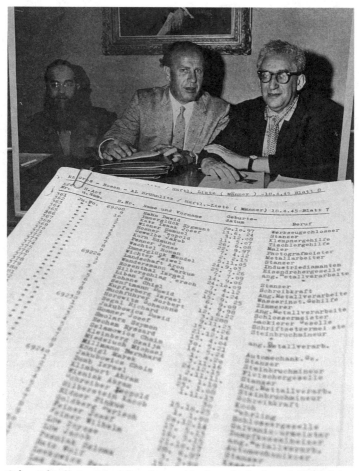

Oskar Schindler's original list, discovered in the attic of a house in Hildesheim in 1999; in the background, a photograph of Oskar Schindler (center)

That is Jennifer Teege's personal German history: her grandfather a Nazi criminal, her grandmother a follower, her mother raised in the leaden silence of the post-war period. That is her family, those are the roots that she, the adopted child, had always been looking for. But what about *her*, where does all that leave her?

■　■　■

MY DISCOVERY LEADS ME TO QUESTION everything that had been central to my life: my close relationships with my adoptive brothers and with my friends in Israel, my marriage, my two sons. Has my whole life been a lie? I feel like I have been traveling under a false name, like I have betrayed everyone, when really it is I who was betrayed. I was the one who was cheated—out of my history, my childhood, my identity.

I no longer know to whom I belong: my adoptive family, or the Goeth family? When I was seven, after the adoption, giving up the name Goeth had seemed easy to do. A document was drawn up. My adoptive parents asked if I was OK with changing my name. I said yes. I didn't venture to ask about my biological mother after that; I wanted a normal family at last. But now it seems I have no choice in the matter: I am a Goeth.

During my Internet research on Amon Goeth, I also learn of a TV program on the culture channel "Arte." An American film-maker has documented a meeting between my mother and Helen Rosenzweig, a former concentration-camp inmate and maid in my grandfather's mansion. As it happens, the film is going to be shown for the first time on German television tomorrow.

First the book, now this film—it's too much, everything is happening too quickly.

My husband and I watch the film together. Right at the beginning, my mother appears. I lean toward the television; I want to see everything clearly: *What does she look like, how does she move, how does she talk? Am I like her?* She has dyed her hair strawberry blonde; she looks haggard. I like the way she expresses herself. When I was a child, she was just my mother to me. Children don't register whether somebody is simple or educated. Now I realize: *My mother is an intelligent woman; she is saying interesting things.*

The documentary also shows a key scene from *Schindler's List*, where the Jewish forewoman explains to the newly appointed commandant Amon Goeth that the barracks have not been planned correctly—so Goeth, played by Ralph Fiennes, has the woman shot. She manages to say, "Herr Commandant, I am only doing my job." And Fiennes, as Goeth, replies, "And I'm doing mine."

My memories of the film are beginning to come back to me. That scene had shocked me, since it shows so clearly what is so difficult to imagine: In the camp, there are no limits and no inhibitions. Common sense and humanity have been abolished.

But what can I, with my dark skin and friends all over the world, have to do with such a grandfather? Was it he who destroyed my family? Did he cast his shadow first on my mother and then on me? Can it be that a dead man still wields power over the living? Is the depression that has plagued me for so long connected to my origins? I lived and studied in Israel for five years—was that chance or fate? Will I have to behave differently toward my Israeli friends, now that I know? *My grandfather murdered your relatives.*

I am dreaming: I am swimming in a dark lake, the water as thick as tar. Suddenly corpses appear all around me: spindly figures, skeletons almost, that have had everything humane taken from them.

Why did my mother not think it necessary to inform me about my origins? Why did she tell others these things that I, too, absolutely needed to know? She never told me the truth. But I need the truth. I am reminded of Theodor W. Adorno's famous phrase, *There is no right life in the wrong one.* He meant it differently when he said it, but it seems to apply perfectly to my life now.

Ours was a difficult relationship: We met only sporadically, but she is still my mother. The book about Monika Goeth mentions the year 1970, the year of my birth. There is not a word about me; my mother pretends I don't exist.

Again and again I look at the picture in the book where she looks just as I remember her from my childhood. Deep inside my head, the drawers of my memory are opening one by one. My entire childhood comes up to the surface, all the feelings from my time in the orphanage, the loneliness and the despair.

I feel helpless again, like a small, disappointed child, and I am losing my grip on life.

All I want to do is sleep; often I stay in bed until midday. Everything feels like too much effort: having to get up, to talk. Even brushing my teeth is a struggle. The answering machine is permanently switched on, but I never manage to return any calls. I stop seeing my friends, and I turn down all invitations. What could I possibly talk or laugh about? It feels as if there is a glass wall between my family and me. How can I explain to them what I am going through, when I myself don't understand what is happening to me?

Suddenly I can no longer bear people drinking beer near me. The smell of beer alone is enough to make me sick: It reminds me of my mother's first husband. When he was drunk, which he usually was, he would beat my mother.

For two weeks after discovering the book, I hardly leave the house. Sometimes I manage to pull on a pair of jeans instead of the usual sweatpants, but I'm soon overwhelmed by crushing tiredness and wonder why I have bothered to shower and get dressed when I am not going out anyway.

My husband does his best to look after our children. He gets the groceries on the weekends, fills up the freezer and cooks meals in advance. I don't want to be a bad mother who just leaves her sons to watch TV in the afternoons. Instead I go online and order some Legos for them; it will keep my children busy for a few hours while I get some rest.

Finally I try once again to go out, to look after my family, but I falter at the smallest hurdles. In the supermarket, the crowds make me nervous. Baffled, I find myself staring at the different types of coffee on the shelf. Surely I have much more urgent business to do at the post office? So I go to the post office instead, but once there I find that the line is too long, and I hurry back to the supermarket, back to the coffee shelf. I remember that I had actually wanted some milk and bread. But much more important is lunch—now where am I going to get that? It is getting late, and I need to go and fetch the children from preschool soon. The pressure is rising, my head is my prison. Once again, I've gotten nothing done.

I never had a real mother myself, and so I've tried to give my children everything I never had, but now I'm deserting them. I make sandwiches for them and heat up TV dinners. Simple, functional things; nothing more. My older son Claudius craves my company. At bedtime, he wants lots of cuddles and talks to me, fast and nonstop, so as not to allow any gaps in the conversation where I might turn away again. I try to concentrate on what he is saying, but I can't. I nod my head every now and then to pretend I am listening. I would love to just pull the blanket over my head.

Why didn't I discover that I am the granddaughter of some great Nobel Prize winner?

■　■　■

Anybody who is related to Joseph Goebbels, Heinrich Himmler, Hermann Goering or an Amon Goeth is compelled to deal with their family history. But what about all the others, the many unnamed followers and accomplices?

In his research study *Grandpa Wasn't a Nazi*, social psychologist Harald Welzer came to the following conclusion: The generation of grandchildren, today's 30- to 50-year olds, tend to know the facts about the Holocaust and often reject the Nazi ideology even more strongly than the previous generation. Their critical eye, however, is only directed at political issues—not at private affairs. The grandchildren in particular sugarcoat the role their ancestors played: Two-thirds of those questioned even stylized their forebears into heroes of the Resistance or victims of the Nazi regime themselves.

Many have no idea what their own grandfathers were really up to. To them, the Holocaust is a history class, the victims' story memorialized in films and on TV; they don't look at it as the history of their own family, their own personal history. So many innocent grandfathers, so many suppressed family secrets. Soon the last witnesses will be gone, and it will be too late for the grandchildren to ask questions.

■　■　■

Amon Goeth in 1945, after his arrest by the Americans

WHEN I LOOKED IN THE MIRROR as a child, it was obvious that I was different: My skin was dark, my hair frizzy. All around me there were only short, blond people: my adoptive parents and my two adoptive brothers. By contrast, I was a tall child with skinny legs and black hair. Back then, in the seventies, I was the only black child in Waldtrudering, the tranquil, leafy neighborhood in Munich where I lived with my adoptive family. At school we sometimes sang the nursery rhyme "Zehn Kleine Negerlein" (Ten little negroes)—and I hoped that nobody would turn around and look at me, that nobody would realize I didn't really belong.

Since that day in the library I have been looking in the mirror again, but now I'm looking for similarities. I'm terrified of belonging now, of belonging to the Goeths: The lines between my nose and my mouth are just like my mother's and my grandfather's. A thought flashes across my mind: I must do something about these lines, must have them botoxed, lasered, lifted!

I am tall like my mother, like my grandfather. When Amon Goeth was hanged after the war, the executioner had to shorten the rope twice; he had underestimated how tall Goeth was.

My grandfather's execution was recorded on film, so there would be proof that he really was dead. It is not until the third attempt that he ends up swinging on the rope with a broken neck. When I watched the film, I didn't know whether to laugh or cry.

My grandfather was a psychopath, a sadist. He embodies everything that I condemn. What kind of person takes pleasure in tormenting and killing others, in inventing different ways of doing so? During my research I find no explanation for why he turned out to be like that. He had seemed normal as a child.

On the matter of blood: What did I inherit from him? Does his violent temper manifest itself in me and my children? In the book about my mother, I read that she spent some time as a patient in a psychiatric hospital. The book also mentions that my grandmother kept small pink pills called Prolixin in her bathroom cabinet. I learn that it is an antipsychotic drug used to treat depression, anxiety disorders, and hallucinations.

I no longer trust myself: Am I going mad, too? Am I already mad? At night I am plagued by terrible nightmares. In one I am in a psychiatric hospital, running through the corridors trying to escape. I jump out of a window into a courtyard and am free at last.

I make an appointment with the therapist who used to treat my depression when I was still living in Munich, and I travel to see her.

Before the appointment, I have some time, so I decide to take a detour to Hasenbergl, the poor neighborhood of Munich where my biological mother used to live. Sometimes she would come and take me home for the weekend. It still looks just as it did then, only the

15

façades of the buildings are more colorful now, the dirty gray and beige walls have been painted yellow and orange. The balconies are strung with laundry; the lawns are littered with trash. I am standing outside the apartment block where my mother used to live when someone comes out of the building and holds the door open for me. I walk up and down the different corridors, trying to remember which floor she used to live on. I think it was the second floor, where I feel a familiar sense of trepidation. I was never happy here.

Next I take the subway to Schwabing, Munich's hip and trendy neighborhood. I walk past the beautiful old church at Josephsplatz and turn into Schwind Strasse. My grandmother's former apartment is in an old, prewar building with a chestnut tree in the courtyard. The front door is open; I climb up the wooden stairs right to the top floor. My grandmother was the first person to give me solace and comfort, but the book has taken away any positive feelings I had for her. Who was this woman who spent a year and a half living with my grandfather in a villa next to the Płaszów concentration camp?

I also have an appointment with Child Protective Services. The social worker is very nice and does her best to help me, but I am only allowed to read part of my file. I ask her if there are any notes in the records indicating that I had any mental disorders as a child.

The thing is, there are things I don't know about myself that others take for granted. If a doctor asked me what illnesses ran in my family, I could never answer that question. Nor do I know if I had a pacifier as a baby, what songs I used to sing along to, or what my first cuddly toy was. I didn't have a mother to ask about these things.

No, says the lady from the agency, *there's no mention of any strange behavior.* I was a normally developed, happy child.

I just about manage to make it to my appointment with my former therapist in time. What I want to know from her is, *What was her diagnosis back then? Was I really just depressed, or did I suffer from a more severe illness? Do I appear lucid to her now?* She reassures me that it really was just that, depression, and that she never diagnosed anything else. She does admit, however, that she is out of her depth with my current situation and so refers me to her Munich-based colleague, Peter Bruendl.

■   ■   ■

Psychoanalyst Peter Bruendl remembers Jennifer Teege well. "There was this confident, tall, beautiful woman who asked very specific questions: How do I deal with my history?" Bruendl, an elderly gentleman with a gray beard and in a black suit, has treated several grandchildren of Nazi criminals in his Munich practice. He says, "Violence and brutalization have a deep impact on the generations that follow. What makes them ill, however, is not the crimes themselves but the silence that surrounds them. There is an unholy conspiracy of silence in perpetrator families, often spanning generations."

Guilt cannot be inherited, but *feelings* of guilt can. The children of perpetrators subconsciously pass their fears and feelings of shame and guilt on to their children, says Bruendl. This affects more families in Germany than one might think.

"Jennifer Teege's case was exceptional because she suffered a double trauma," Bruendl says, "first being given up for adoption and then the discovery of her family history."

He goes on, "Frau Teege's experience is heartbreaking. Even her conception was a provocation: Her mother, Monika Goeth, had a child with a Nigerian man. In Munich in the early 1970s, this was most unusual. And for the daughter of a concentration camp commandant it was unheard of."

Often, the grandchildren of Nazis come to him for totally different reasons, says Bruendl: depression, unwanted childlessness, eating disorders, or fear of failure at work. Bruendl encourages them to research their past and to tear down their family's web of lies. "It is only then that they can live their own lives, their own, authentic lives."

■   ■   ■

HERR BRUENDL REFERS ME to the Institute for Psychiatry at the University Hospital in Hamburg. Yet the expert he recommends is not available right away, and with every day that I have to wait I grow more and more desperate. I know that I need professional help and that everybody else is unsure how to deal with me. Sometimes I lose my temper and shout at Goetz and the children. I cannot pull myself together, cannot hold myself together anymore.

One morning, when I start to cry just after getting up, my sons ask me, *Mommy, what's wrong?*

Nothing, I answer—and then take myself to the psychiatric emergency room at the local University Hospital. The doctor on duty prescribes me antidepressants, and I take them straight away.

During the following weeks I feel like I have been superficially restored to my usual self. Then, at last, I have my appointment with the recommended therapist. His professor's office, where we meet, may be austere, but he understands my internal suffering. When he hears my story, he cries with me, and I feel in safe hands with him. My therapist will not cry with me again, but he will take good care of me in the coming months.

I start running again. I have always enjoyed my own company—traveling alone, running alone. One of my favorite places to run is a small wooded area in Hamburg. I start in the cool shade of the trees, and continue along fields and past paddocks with horses in them. I run through community gardens with garden gnomes among the flowerbeds: This pointedly idyllic world has something touching about it, and afterward my head feels clearer.

My adoptive family still don't know; I will tell them at Christmas, when we all come together at their house in Munich.

My Christmas present to everyone is a copy of the book about my mother, plus the only biography ever written of Amon Goeth. It is a hefty volume, authored by a Viennese historian.

My adoptive parents, Inge and Gerhard—I cannot call them Mama and Papa anymore—are surprised and shocked. When I discovered the book, I had first suspected that they knew everything about my biological family but that they had wanted to protect me, that they, too, had betrayed me. Yet I soon realized that they would never have kept anything so fundamental hidden from me. Their reaction now tells me that I was right: They knew nothing either.

My adoptive parents have always struggled to talk about feelings, and now it is no different. They escape into academic details: *Amon Goeth's biography has no footnotes,* my father complains, and then asks, *Does the number of dead correspond with other sources?* My life has been turned upside down, and my adoptive parents are discussing footnotes! My brothers, on the other hand, understand straight away what this book means to me.

■   ■   ■

Jennifer Teege's adoptive mother clearly remembers the moment when Jennifer was sitting on the sofa that Christmas Eve, struggling for words. "Jenny announced that there was something important that she wanted

19

to talk about. But then she just looked at us and started welling up. I sensed that something bad had happened." When Inge Sieber had heard the whole story, she didn't know how to deal with it at first. "My husband and I felt as if somebody had pulled the rug out from under our feet."

Jennifer Teege's adoptive brother Matthias couldn't sleep that Christmas night. "I was worried about how the discovery would affect Jenny. With this book, a different world had opened up for her. She had found her other self; she had seen where she had come from. She had spent a lot of time dealing with who her grandfather was, and even more so with the women in her family, her mother and her grandmother."

Suddenly, Jennifer regarded herself less as the daughter of her adoptive parents; instead she saw herself as part of her natural family. Matthias thinks that this upset his parents very much.

He himself was very worried about his sister: "She was so gloomy, so depressed, like I had never seen her before. I had always thought she was so strong. She was always the boldest, the most daring of us three children."

■ ■ ■

IN THE FOLLOWING MONTHS, my brother Matthias turns into my most important confidant, after my husband. In his research, he digs up more and more details about the Goeth family.

My Israeli friends Noa and Anat keep sending me emails: *Jenny, where are you, what's going on?* I have neither the strength nor the words to reply. I don't want to hurt my friends' feelings. I can't remember exactly where they lost their relatives during the Holocaust. I'll have to ask them—but what if they say, *In Płaszów?*

The thing is, Amon Goeth's victims are not abstract figures to me, not just an anonymous crowd. When I think of them, I see the faces of the elderly people I met during my studies in Israel at the Goethe Institute. They were Holocaust survivors who wanted to hear and speak German again, the language of their old home country. Some could not see very well, so I read German newspapers and novels to them. On their forearms I could see their prisoners' numbers from the camps tattooed on their skin. For the first time my German nationality felt wrong, like something I had to apologize for. Luckily I was well camouflaged—thanks to my dark skin, nobody suspected that I was German.

How would those survivors have reacted if they had known that I was Amon Goeth's granddaughter? Maybe they would have wanted nothing to do with me. Maybe they would have seen him in me.

My husband tells me, *Go and find your mother's address and confront her with your anger and your questions. And tell your friends in Israel why you haven't been in touch.*

Not yet, I reply. I need to think first. And I have to visit some graves. In Krakow.

CHAPTER 2

MASTER OF THE PŁASZÓW CONCENTRATION CAMP:

MY GRANDFATHER AMON GOETH

If he liked you, you lived, if he didn't, you were dead.

—MIETEK PEMPER, FORMER ASSISTANT TO AMON GOETH

CAREFULLY I PLACE ONE FOOT in front of the other. The floor beneath me sways; the rotten wood creaks and yields under the pressure of each step. It is cold and damp in here; the air smells musty. It's such a squalid place. What's that over there? Is that rat droppings? There is no proper light in here; not enough light, and not enough air either. Carefully I continue walking through my grandfather's house, crossing the dark fishbone parquet into the former trophy room. Amon Goeth once had a sign put up here that said HE WHO SHOOTS FIRST LIVES LONGER.

I had wanted to see the house where my grandparents lived. A Polish tour guide whose address I found on the Internet told me that it still stood. A pensioner lives there now, and every now and then he shows individual visitors around. The tour guide called the man and arranged for me to see the house.

In the Płaszów neighborhood of Krakow, the only dilapidated house on quiet Heltmana Street stands out like a sore thumb against the other neat and tidy single-family homes. Some of its window-panes are broken; the curtains are dirty; the house looks unlived-in. A large sign on the front of the house says SPRZEDAM. FOR SALE.

The front door still looks beautiful; the wood is decorated with ornaments, and the dark red paint has faded only a little. An unkempt man opens the door and leads me up a narrow stairway into the house. My tour guide Malgorzata Kieres—she's asked me to call her by her first name—translates his Polish for me. I haven't told Malgorzata why I am interested in the house; she thinks I am a tourist with a general interest in history.

I look around. The plaster is coming off the walls. There is hardly any furniture. But there is a coldness that creeps into your bones. And a stench. The ceilings are underpinned with wooden beams. I hope the house won't collapse on top of me and bury me beneath it.

Crumbling walls, holding up the past.

Over a year has gone by since I first found the book about my mother in the library. Since then I have read everything I could find about my grandfather and the Nazi era. I am haunted by the thought of him, I think about him constantly. Do I see him as a grandfather or as a historical character? He is both to me: Płaszów commandant Amon Goeth, and my grandfather.

When I was young I was very interested in the Holocaust. I went on a school trip from Munich to the Dachau concentration camp, and I devoured one book about the Nazi era after another, such as *When Hitler Stole Pink Rabbit, A Square of Sky,* and Anne Frank's *Diary of a Young Girl.* I saw the world through Anne Frank's eyes; I felt her fear but also her optimism and her hope.

The history teachers at my high school showed us documentaries about the liberation of the concentration camps, and we saw people who had been reduced to mere skeletons. I read book after book, looking for answers, to find out what drove the perpetrators to act the way they did, but in the end I gave up: Yes, I found some explanations, but I would never understand it completely. Finally, finished with the subject, I concluded that I would have behaved differently. I was different; today's Germans were different.

When I first arrived in Israel in my early twenties, I picked up books about Nazism again. Yet even there, where I was meeting the victims and their children and grandchildren on a daily basis, more important issues soon took over. I had read so much and asked so many people about it—I felt like I knew everything there was to know about the Holocaust. I was much more interested in the here and now: the Palestinian conflict, the threat of war.

I had thought I knew it all, but now, at nearly 40, I have to start all over.

One of the first books I pick up is a classic from 1967, *The Inability to Mourn* by Alexander and Margarete Mitscherlich. I like their approach; they look deep inside each person and try to understand without judgment. In their role as psychoanalysts, they regularly dealt with patients who were active members of the SS or other Nazi organizations before 1945. These people did not appear to have any sense of remorse or shame; they and their fellow Germans continued to live their lives as if the Third Reich had never existed. Reading the book with the knowledge of my family history, I think of my grandmother, who denied Amon Goeth's actions until the end.

The conclusion the Mitscherlichs drew at the end of the 1960s was that the Germans had denied their past and suppressed their guilt; ideally, the whole nation should have been in therapy. That conclusion no longer applies to today's Germans.

I also read books by other Nazi descendants, for example by Richard von Schirach, son of Reich Youth Leader Baldur von Schirach, and by Katrin Himmler, great-niece of Heinrich Himmler,

Reich Leader of the SS. Their family histories are of great interest to me, and I look for similarities.

I begin to dig deeper, I question family and friends. My adoptive mother's stepfather in Vienna, for example, served in Africa under Erwin Rommel. On long mountain walks he would tell us children anecdotes from that time, thrilling adventure stories of valiant warriors fighting in the desert, stories of how they collected the early morning dew from the tent sheets for drinking water, or how they once had to dig their car out of the sand dunes. At first we thought that our "Opa Vienna," as we used to call him, was Rommel's personal driver, but he put us right: He was only one of the drivers in the German Africa Corps. One day "the Limey got him," and he would tell us stories in his Viennese dialect about his time as a prisoner of war.

He only told us one horror story from the war: A soldier had been murdered—beheaded—and afterward his decapitated body was still running around like a headless chicken. That story always gave us the creeps.

When it came to talking about his superior, Opa only had words of praise. Rommel, the sly Desert Fox, was a "decent" Nazi? An urban legend. What skeletons are my adoptive family hiding in the closet?

Memories of discussions with my adoptive father are coming back to me. He was a liberal, often volunteered his services to friends and neighbors, and played an active part in the peace movement. On the subject of the Holocaust, however, he could not let go of the question of whether the number of murdered Jews was really accurate, or if it hadn't been less. He and his friends would argue fiercely about it. My adoptive brothers and I found the discussion unnecessary and didn't understand why this issue was so important to our father.

Suddenly I am not so sure anymore: Am I really so different? Have we really left everything behind us? What does it mean for me, for our time, that my grandfather was a war criminal?

My perception of time is changing. Events that happened a very long time ago are suddenly feeling very recent again. In the last few months I have read so much, have watched so many films; everything seems so immediate. Maybe it's because, to me, this old story is now very new, very fresh. Often, when I delve into this world my grandfather inhabited, it feels as if these crimes happened only yesterday.

And now I am standing here in this dilapidated villa in Krakow. I am not quite sure what I'm doing here, in this house, in this city. Does being here make any sense at all? I just know that I had needed to come to Krakow now. Shortly before I came I was in the hospital—I'd had a miscarriage.

I am feeling sad and exhausted. My therapist advised me not to travel to Krakow in my condition, but I had really wanted to make this trip. First I flew to Warsaw and then I took the train on to Krakow, the city where my grandfather was infamous, where it rained ashes at the end of the war when he had the remains of thousands of people cremated.

I want to see where my grandfather committed his murders. I want to get close to him—and then put some distance between him and me.

On the ground floor, the old man is now showing me the living room. This is where the parties were held, he says with a sweep of his arm. Here they sat, my grandfather and the other Nazis, drinking schnapps and wine. Oskar Schindler was there, too. The old man leads me onto the patio. He explains that my grandfather had some building work done, had balconies and patios added. The view of the countryside was important to him, he says.

Amon Goeth's former commandant's villa in Płaszów in 1995

The house must have been beautiful once; I like the style. Did my grandfather redesign the building himself? Was he interested in architecture like me? Why am I even thinking about whether we share the same tastes? Amon Goeth is not the kind of grandfather you want to find similarities with. The crimes he committed override everything else. In the book about my mother, I read that my grandmother used to gush about Amon Goeth's table manners, even long after the war was over. He was a real gentleman, she said.

■　■　■

A concentration camp commandant who set great store by table manners.

Emilie Schindler, Oskar Schindler's wife, later said about Amon Goeth that he had a "split personality." "On the one hand he played the gentleman, like every man from Vienna; on the other he subjected the Jews under his control to unrelenting terror. . . . He could kill people in cold blood and yet notice any false note on the classical records he played endlessly."

Amon Leopold Goeth was born in Vienna on December 11, 1908, the only child of a Catholic family of publishers. His parents Bertha and Amon Franz Goeth named him after his father and grandfather: Amon. In ancient Egypt, Amon was the ram-headed god of fertility. In Hebrew, Amon means *son of my people*. In the Old Testament, Amon was a king of Judaea who worshipped pagan gods and was killed by his servants.

Amon Goeth's parents came from a humble background but had come into money with their bookselling business. They could afford to live in a middle-class neighborhood, have a maid and eventually own a car, too. The Goeths sold religious literature, icons, and picture postcards. Later on they expanded into publishing, producing books about military history which mourned the Germans lost to World War I. Amon Goeth's father was often away traveling for the business while his mother managed the shop, and as a young boy Amon was often looked after by his childless aunt.

Amon, or "Mony" as he was often called, went to a private Catholic elementary school. He wasn't a very good student. His parents eventually sent him to a strict Catholic boarding school in the country. His biographer, historian Johannes Sachslehner, suggests that Goeth's future "tendency to play strange sadistic jokes" might stem from experiences he had during this time, but there is no evidence to support this claim.

Amon Goeth left the boarding school at the end of tenth grade against his parents' wishes. At 17 he was already enthralled by radical right wing ideas and had joined fascist youth organizations. He was athletic and reckless—characteristics that impressed his new friends.

In 1931 he became a member of the NSDAP, the National Socialist German Workers' Party, or Nazi party for short, and soon after he joined their security force, the SS.

Heinrich Himmler's SS, also responsible for experiments on humans and mass murder in the concentration camps, was regarded as the elite unit: "The best of the best, you couldn't be more Nazi if you tried," journalist Stephen Lebert once described the spirit of this corps in a nutshell. Hans Egon Holthusen wrote, in his 1966 confessional autobiography *Volunteering for the SS*, "This organization with their black uniform and death-head emblem was seen as elite, chic and elegant, which is why it was the organization of choice for the privileged youths who considered themselves too posh to go running around in the 'shitty-brown colored' outfit of the SA, the storm battalion."

The young Amon Goeth, unsuccessful at school and constantly pressured by his parents, was among those drawn to the idea of belonging to an elite. Later he would tell his live-in lover Ruth Irene Kalder that his parents had neglected him as a child and that he had turned his back on the middle-class values that they had tried to instill in him. It is true he returned to the family business for a short period of time, successfully publishing military history with his father. He even married a woman his parents introduced him to, although he wasn't in love. This "arranged marriage" soon ended in divorce.

An SS man has to start a family though, so Goeth married for a second time, this time to Anna Geiger, a sporty girl from Tyrol whom he had met at a motorcycle race. Since the aim of the marriage was above all the conception of healthy, "Aryan" offspring, the pair had to undergo a number of tests for the SS. For example, they had to have their pictures taken wearing only swimsuits to demonstrate their physical flawlessness. They were married by an SS man. Anna soon gave birth to a son, but the baby died after just a few months.

Shortly afterward, in March 1940, Amon Goeth reported for duty with the Waffen-SS, the military arm of the SS, and left Vienna for Poland. He was ambitious and climbed the ranks quickly. At first he was only charged with administrative tasks. An appraisal from 1941 states that he was an "SS man willing to make sacrifices, fit for service," "SS leadership material," and that the "overall racial image" was there, too. In 1942, in the Polish city of Lublin, Amon Goeth was given orders to establish labor camps to accommodate Jewish forced laborers.

In 1943, Heinrich Himmler delivered his infamous speech in front of top SS officials where he propagandized an ideology of hatred and contempt: "Whether other nations are living in prosperity or are starving to death interests me only insofar as we need them as slaves for our culture. . . . Whether or not 10,000 Russian women die of exhaustion during the construction of an anti-tank ditch interests me only insofar as the ditch is being finished. I also want to mention . . . a very difficult subject here. . . . I am talking about the evacuation of the Jews, the extermination of the Jewish people. . . . Most of you will know what it is like when 100 bodies are piled up together, when there are 500 or when there are 1,000. To have seen this through and to have stayed decent—with the exception of human weaknesses—that is what has made us tough."

Amon Goeth soon went on to prove his toughness. The SS taught him how to kill.

■　　■　　■

UPSTAIRS, THE OLD MAN UNLOCKS the door to the former bedroom. There are hooks in the ceiling. *This is where Amon Goeth did his exercises,* the old man claims. *Or maybe,* he adds with a wink, *he had a love-swing hanging from there.*

I step onto the balcony and look out over the hills covered in brushwood. A cold wind blows in my face. It is a rainy October day. The camp, surrounded by barbed wire and guarded by watchtowers, was located near the house. My grandfather could keep an eye on his prisoners; in the mornings it was only a short walk to work. That blurred photograph of Amon Goeth on the cover of the book about my mother—his open mouth, the bare chest, the rifle in his hand, wearing only shorts on his balcony—who took that photo? Was it my grandmother? Amon Goeth is said to have been proud of his firearms; he liked to carry them around with him. Did that impress my grandmother, or did it frighten her? What did she know? What did she suppress? I cannot imagine her living in this house, yet not being aware of what was happening in the camp. Amon Goeth is said to have beaten his maids. My grandmother must have seen or at least heard that, too. The house isn't that big.

After my arrival in Krakow the previous night, on my way to the hotel, I drove past Wawel Castle, the former residence of the kings of Poland, high above the Vistula. The castle was brightly lit. After the German invasion, Hans Frank, Hitler's governor of Poland, made himself at home there, living a life of luxury surrounded by servants, employing composers and chess players. I can imagine the life he had up there, how powerful he must have felt residing in that grand castle with its view over Krakow.

By comparison Amon Goeth's house looks very normal, almost modest. I had imagined it to be bigger, more ostentatious. I find it difficult to imagine that glamorous receptions were held here and that its owner was a man who was master of life and death for thousands of people. A man who thrived on having absolute power, and who wielded and relished this power in the most cynical way absolutely.

■　■　■

Amon Goeth on the balcony of his villa

"I am your God," said Amon Goeth to the prisoners in his inaugural address as commandant of the Płaszów camp. "I dispatched 60,000 Jews in the district of Lublin. Now it's your turn."

In the Polish city of Lublin, Amon Goeth had worked for Odilo Globocnik, an SS man known for his brutality, whom Heinrich Himmler had charged with killing the Jews in occupied Poland. In December 1940, Globocnik updated Hans Frank on the goal he had set out with these words: "In this one year, I have obviously not been able to eradicate all the lice and all the Jews. But I am convinced that in the course of time it can be achieved. . . ."

When the "Final Solution" was being strategically coordinated at the Wannsee Conference on January 20, 1942, the deportation and mass murder of Polish Jews was already in full swing.

Goeth's superior Odilo Globocnik was co-responsible for the construction of concentration camps and the installation of gas chambers. In consultation with Adolf Eichmann he planned the factory-style murder of millions of people. In Poland, extermination camps were being commissioned: Belzec, Sobibor, Treblinka.

Soon Odilo Globocnik charged Amon Goeth with the liquidation of the ghettos. Liquidation meant rounding up the able ghetto population into forced labor; those too weak or too ill to work were shot, including children and the elderly. Historian Johannes Sachslehner describes the process as "blood-thirsty manhunts following a proven formula. . . . In the thick of it is Amon Goeth, who is soon entrusted with leading roles."

If he hadn't done so already, Goeth surely now discovered the lucrative side of genocide: Jews who offered him valuables such as furs, fine china, or jewelry were not killed immediately but were "allowed" to go to the labor camps.

Around this time Amon Goeth also started to drink more and more heavily.

Soon the ambitious Goeth was given more tasks: He was to lead the liquidation of the Krakow ghetto and establish a forced labor camp in Płaszów. In letters to his friends and to his father in Vienna he said, "Now I am the commandant at last."

On March 13 and 14, 1943, he ordered the clearance of the Krakow ghetto. Around 2,000 people are killed during these two days; a further 4,000 are deported, many to Auschwitz.

The survivors were taken to Amon Goeth's realm: Płaszów. Almost 200 acres in size, the camp was first a labor camp and later a concentration camp. The German occupiers had built it on Jewish cemeteries. They built barracks on top of the demolished graves and used the gravestones to pave the streets in the camp.

■　■　■

THE OLD MAN LEADS ME into the basement. "This is where the commandant stored his wine," he says. And then he points proudly to a rusty tub: "Amon Goeth's authentic bathtub."

Opposite the wine cellar and next to the kitchen was the maids' room. So this was Helen's place, here in the basement—Helen Rosenzweig, Amon Goeth's former Jewish maid from the American documentary I watched on TV the day after I discovered the book.

My mother met Helen here in this house. Ultimately it was a very sad encounter: Helen was shocked because my mother had such a striking resemblance to Amon Goeth. And even though Helen and my mother both try very hard, they cannot form a relationship with each other; history stands between them. Helen sees Amon Goeth in my mother.

In the film, when my mother tries to find an explanation for Amon Goeth's actions, Helen snaps angrily: "He was a monster. He was smiling and whistling when he came back from killing. He had the urge to kill, like an animal. It was obvious."

My brother Matthias has given me the documentary on DVD so that I can watch it again and again. At first I focused only on my mother and didn't pay much attention to Helen. The film begins with my mother writing a letter to Helen asking her for a meeting. In the letter she says that she imagines Helen might be afraid of meeting her—she herself is scared to meet Helen.

At the start, I wasn't so concerned about the actual contents of the letter. All I could think was, why does my mother spend so much time writing a letter to Helen? Why doesn't she write to me? Why does she share Helen's pain but not that of her own child?

Then gradually my feelings faded into the background and suddenly I saw Helen. I saw her, after all those years, returning anxiously to this house that used to be her dreadful prison. I saw how she is still plagued by her memories. She recounts how Amon Goeth used to beat the maids, how he pushed them down these very stairs, how he screamed at them and called them *slut, bitch, dirty Jewess.*

Helen's boyfriend was a member of the Jewish Resistance in the camp and was shot by Goeth. Helen also talks about the man she loved after the war, a camp survivor like herself. They were married for 35 years, moved to Florida and had children. Yet her husband could not get over the experience of the camp, and one day he took his own life. In his suicide note he wrote, "The memories haunt me every day. I just can't go on."

I am standing in the basement of my grandfather's house, in the darkness of Helen's room, where the only light comes from a small window. You can see a small patch of the garden. It was warm here; she didn't have to sleep on straw in the drafty barracks and was certain to have had more to eat than the other detainees. She didn't have to perform hard labor in the quarries like most of the other women in the camp; she wore a black dress with a white apron and served roast meat and wine. Yet she was living beneath the same roof as the man who could kill her at any time. She expected to die in this house.

■   ■   ■

When you saw Goeth, you saw death, one survivor said. The Płaszów camp became the stage for Amon Goeth's cruelty.

There are many eyewitness reports relating to this. Goeth's Jewish assistant, Mietek Pemper, described how once, in the middle of a dictation, the commandant suddenly grabbed his rifle, opened a window, and started shooting at prisoners. Pemper heard screams; Goeth then returned to his desk and asked calmly, as if nothing had happened, *Where were we?*

When Amon Goeth killed somebody, he would have their relatives killed, too, because he didn't want to see any "unhappy" faces in his camp.

In her memoirs, Płaszów survivor Stella Müller-Madej writes about Goeth, "If there was somebody he didn't like the look of, he'd grab him by the hair and shoot him on the spot. He was a giant of a man, a powerful, imposing figure with beautiful, gentle features and an even gentler expression on his face. So this is what a cruel, murdering monster looks like! How can that be?"

Goeth used publicly celebrated executions to crush any thought of escape or resistance the detainees might have had. Public hangings and shootings on the parade ground were accompanied by popular music. Larger groups of people were usually shot on a hill a little further away; the pit for the bodies was just below.

The Płaszów camp was growing, and the prisoners were now coming from further afield. Survivors from other ghettos, Polish prisoners, Romany from other camps, as well as Hungarian Jews all joined the Jews from the Krakow ghetto. Sometimes the Płaszów concentration camp held more than 20,000 detainees in its 180 barracks surrounded by two and half miles of barbed wire.

Within the SS, Amon Goeth was promoted to the rank of *Hauptsturmführer*, captain, which was an extraordinarily fast rise. He got rich on the prisoners' possessions and lived a life of luxury. He had a Jewish cobbler make new shoes for him every week and a pastry chef bake fancy cakes for him until he was piling on the pounds. In his villa, he held parties; alcohol, music, and women were offered in abundance to humor the SS men. Goeth owned riding horses and a number of cars; he enjoyed riding through the camp on his white horse or racing around the lanes in his BMW.

Mietek Pemper, the commandant's assistant, also took dictation of

Goeth's personal letters to his family in Vienna. Omitting the details of everyday life in the camp, he would ask his father about the progress of the business and his wife about the children: Anna Goeth had given birth to two more children, Ingeborg and Werner. When Amon Goeth learned that Werner was hitting his sister Ingeborg, he told Pemper to write in his letter to his wife Anna: "He must have got the hitting from me."

Eyewitnesses reported that Goeth would wear different accessories depending on his mood on a given day. If he put on white gloves or a white scarf, combined with a peaked cap or a Tyrolean hat, the detainees had to expect the worst. His two dogs, a Great Dane and an Alsatian mix, were called Rolf and Ralf, and he trained them to attack people on his command.

In 1944, Amon Goeth had children from the Płaszów camp herded onto trucks—to be transported to the gas chambers at Auschwitz. He ordered waltz music to be played over the loudspeakers in order to drown out the desperate cries of their parents.

In other words: Amon Goeth was perfect Hollywood material. Just as Adolf Eichmann was for many years the epitome of the callous, bureaucratic mastermind behind the scenes, denying any responsibility, Amon Goeth serves as the grotesquely excessive personification of the sadistic murderer. The image of the trigger-happy concentration camp commandant, accompanied by his two dogs trained to tear humans apart—it seems like a grim archetype, like a template for Paul Celan's poem *Death Fugue*. Steven Spielberg portrays Amon Goeth as a twisted psychopath, cruel, and at the same time almost laughable.

Other, big- and small-screen documentaries about Amon Goeth are often accompanied by ominous background music, but actually his crimes don't call for any embellishment.

Amon Goeth's crimes were so reprehensible that it seems easy enough to distance oneself from them. In his dissertation about concentration camp commandants, the Israeli historian and journalist Tom Segev writes:

Goeth would often ride around the camp on his white horse

"They were by no means Germans like all the other Germans, not even Nazis like all the other Nazis. They are not characterized by the banality of evil, but much more so by their inner identification with this evil. Most of the concentration camp commandants joined the Nazi movement in its early days . . . ; they had been vehement supporters of these radical rightwing politics right from its beginnings. The majority of Germans never even joined the Nazi party."

But Segev's theory might be too simple after all: The late Marcel Reich-Ranicki, literary critic and Holocaust survivor, had good reason to oppose the fact that famous Nazis such as Adolf Hitler are usually portrayed purely as monsters. "Of course Hitler was a human being," Reich-Ranicki said, adding, "What else would he have been? An elephant?"

It is very easy to demonize the prominent Nazis, to treat them like animals in a zoo: Look, aren't they cruel and perverted? It offers a way out of having to deal with one's own actions, one's family's actions—or indeed those of the many people who joined in on a small scale, those who no longer greeted their Jewish neighbors, and those who looked away and walked past when Jews were being beaten up in the streets and their businesses were destroyed.

■ ■ ■

THEY CALLED GOETH THE "BUTCHER OF PŁASZÓW." I keep on asking myself how it was that he became that way. I don't think that it was his childhood or even his hatred of the Jews. I think it was much more banal than that: In this world of men, killing was a contest, a kind of sport. It reached the point where killing a human being meant nothing more than swatting a fly. In the end the mind goes completely numb; death has entertainment value.

I have a terrible image in my head, which used to haunt me even in my sleep: It is said that Amon Goeth once caught a Jewish woman who was boiling potatoes in a large trough for the pigs— just as she, driven by hunger, ate one of the potatoes herself. He shot her in the head and ordered two men to throw the dying woman into the boiling water with the potatoes. One of them refused, so Goeth shot him, too. I don't know if this story is true or not, but I cannot get the image of this half-dead woman thrashing around in the boiling water out of my head.

These stories of how Amon Goeth considered himself superior, how he played music to accompany executions, used scarves and hats as props for his killings, how he played the master in his pathetic little villa—it would be comical if it wasn't so sad. He was a narcissist—but not just in the sense that he was in love with himself. He was a narcissist who felt on top of the world when he humiliated and degraded others.

I read that my grandmother used to idolize him: handsome Amon Goeth, the man of her dreams.

This is juxtaposed to the image of him that contemporary witnesses have painted: quick-tempered, cruel, irascible. His dogs. His exaggerated masculinity: commanding, dominating. Uniform, discipline, Fatherland.

My mother always saw the father in him, too, not just the concentration camp commandant. She is much closer to him than I am, even though she never met him. She was still a baby when he was hanged. Survivors of the camp have told her again and again how much she looks like him. How dreadful that must have been for her.

Do I look like him? My skin color is like a barrier between us. I imagine myself standing next to him. We are both tall: I am six foot, he was six foot four—a giant in those days.

He in his black uniform with its death-heads, me the black grandchild. What would he have said to a dark-skinned granddaughter, who speaks Hebrew on top of that? I would have been a disgrace, a bastard who brought dishonor to the family. I am sure my grandfather would have shot me.

My grandmother was never bothered by my skin color. She always seemed delighted to see me when I came to visit. No matter how little I was at the time: Children can sense if someone likes them, and she liked me. I've always felt so close to her. Yet she also held Amon Goeth when he came back from his killings. How could she share her bed and her home with him? She said she loved him, but is that a good enough excuse? Is it good enough for me? Was there anything loveable about Amon Goeth—is that even a permissible question?

When I look in the mirror I see two faces, mine and his. And a third, my mother's.

The three of us have the same determined chin, the same lines between the nose and the mouth.

Height, lines—those things are only external. But what about on the inside? How much of Amon Goeth do I have in me? How much of Amon Goeth does each of us have in us?

I think we all have a bit of him in us. To believe that I have more than others would be to think like a Nazi—to believe in the power of blood.

The quiet in the villa is suddenly broken: Malgorzata, the Polish woman who interprets the old man's Polish for me, reveals out of the blue that she once met Amon Goeth's daughter Monika. I ask her to tell me more and she says that my mother once came to visit the villa with a group of Polish schoolchildren. They were accompanied by a descendant of another Nazi, Niklas Frank, son of Hans Frank, governor-general of Hitler's occupied Poland.

Since Malgorzata doesn't know who I am I ask her what she thought of my mother. "I thought she was a bit strange, and sad," she replies. "Niklas Frank and Monika Goeth, neither of them could laugh." And then she tells us that here in this house Monika Goeth had touched a doorpost and said that she loved her father.

My mother's hand on the door. There are hundreds of German-speaking tour guides in Krakow, and I chose the one who has met my mother.

I tell Malgorzata who I am. At first she doesn't believe me, then she becomes bewildered and confused. I apologize to her. In order to find out more about my mother I had asked questions without revealing my identity. I say that I hope she understands my situation.

I had been determined to contact my mother before the end of the year. Now the year is almost over—it is well into fall, but I don't want to write to my mother until I feel better prepared for it.

In the documentary about her meeting with Amon Goeth's former maid Helen, my mother frequently cries. I can see the strain she's under because of her father's past. Krakow has a special meaning for her. I thought that I'd be able to understand my mother better if I, too, got to know this place.

The old man shows Malgorzata and me out. I pull the door firmly shut behind me.

There's another tour I've booked in Krakow: a *Schindler's List* tour.

I take a taxi to the meeting place in Kazimierz, the former Jewish quarter of Krakow. In the summer, Kazimierz is meant to be picturesque and charming; but today it seems dark and gloomy. The cobblestones are wet with rain. Our group of tourists visits the old Jewish cemetery, a synagogue, and a few locations from *Schindler's List*. We see idyllic courtyards and narrow alleys.

Many restaurants in Kazimierz serve gefilte fish and kosher meat. Pretty little cafés play traditional klezmer music—the rhythm of a long-lost time—around the clock. There is a morbid, museum-like feel to the whole district.

The narrow little alleys and the rough paving stones remind me of Mea Shearim, the Orthodox Jewish quarter of Jerusalem. The difference is, Jews actually live in Mea Shearim. Our tour guide tells us that before World War II there were 70,000 Jews in Krakow. Now there are only a few hundred. Most of the Jewish people walking through Kazimierz these days are visitors. There are six tourists in my group; I want to know where they are from. The response: Poland, USA, France. They want to know where I come from. "Germany," I say. "Ah!" they reply. I am glad we are not wearing name badges.

I still haven't really told anybody about my family history, apart from my husband, my adoptive family, and a close friend. Not because I think I need to be ashamed of it, but because I don't know how to deal with it. I find it hard to share my discovery. How could I put it? "Oh, by the way, I'm the granddaughter of a mass murderer"? I can't cope with my background myself, and I don't want to burden anybody else with it either. Not yet anyway.

Our small group moves on; we go over a little bridge across the Vistula river to the neighboring district of Podgorze. This is where the entire Jewish population of Krakow was crammed into a ghetto. The trams still ran through the middle of it, taking the people of Krakow across their city. Inside the ghetto, nobody was allowed to get in or out of the tram; there were no stops, and the doors and windows were locked for the duration. I wonder how the people of Krakow felt when they traveled through here.

Today a large office building stands in the square that used to be the center of the ghetto, and there is a bus depot, too. On the edge, a few sections of the ghetto walls remain. To add insult to injury, these tall walls surrounding the people behind them had arches at the top—they were built in the shape of Jewish tombstones. The message to the Jews was clear: You won't get out alive.

The victims are remembered at Ghetto Heroes Square. Empty, larger-than-life chairs dotted around the square are meant to convey a sense of the devastation in the ghetto after it had been liquidated: Everything laid to waste, no people in the streets, only furniture and other personal possessions that the Jews had been forced to leave behind. I find the installation too cold, too conceptual. Hundreds of people were killed during the clearing of the ghetto. Every chair represents 1,000 Jews who were murdered. The brutalities that were committed here remain abstract. But how can they be displayed? *Schindler's List* is very graphic, but survivors say that even Spielberg's film barely hints at the real horror that emanated from Amon Goeth.

■　■　■

Tadeusz Pankiewicz, a Polish druggist in the Krakow ghetto, described Goeth as a tall, handsome man with blue eyes, dressed in a black leather coat and carrying a riding crop. Survivors reported that during the liquidation of the ghetto Goeth tore little children from their mothers' arms and flung them to the ground.

Before the liquidation, 20,000 people were living in the ghetto in cramped conditions and in constant fear of death.

When Amon Goeth had the ghetto cleared on March 13 and 14, 1943, it had already been divided into two separate areas: Ghetto A was for

In front of the walls of the former Jewish ghetto in Krakow

those who had been declared fit for work and who were to be transported to the Płaszów camp; they were allowed to live for now. Ghetto B, separated from Ghetto A by barbed wire, was for the old, the young, and the ill; they were going to be killed.

Nobody was to get away. Goeth's people combed through all the alleys, looked in every apartment and under every bed. In the hospitals, the patients were shot in their beds. Tadeusz Pankiewicz described the scene of the aftermath like this: "It looks like a battlefield—thousands of abandoned bundles and suitcases . . . on pavements drenched in blood."

■ ■ ■

WE MOVE ON. IT IS RAINING, and we have to keep looking for shelter. A nice, elderly lady lets me share her umbrella. We walk beneath a drafty underpass and enter an industrial park. We stop in front of a gray, three-story office block dating from the 1930s: Oskar Schindler's former enamelware factory on Lipowa Street.

Today it has been turned into a museum dedicated to his memory. We visit the exhibition. It starts with photographs of Krakow in the early 1930s. There are women going for their daily walk and men on their way to synagogue. Then follows a portrayal of the German blitzkrieg against Poland and the immediate ostracism of the Jews. One picture shows German soldiers cutting off the sidelocks of an Orthodox Jew with a knife.

I am tired and worn out. I've been on my feet since the early morning. I would love to just sit down somewhere and get some rest, but the tour guide keeps on talking. I am losing my concentration and can no longer remember any of the details.

In the last room of the museum there is a recreation of the Płaszów camp. Little model barracks, even my grandfather's villa.

I take a close look: Again it is obvious how close Goeth's villa was to the camp and the prisoners' barracks. I find my grandmother's justifications less and less credible.

The exhibition covers Oskar Schindler, the man, only marginally. His story is told by means of photographs, documents, and his original furniture. In one room there is a large transparent cube filled with tin pots, bowls, and plates that were produced in his factory during the war. The installation is meant to symbolize the history of Schindler and his workers. Inside the cube are the names of the 1,200 Jewish slave laborers whose lives Oskar Schindler saved.

At the end of the exhibition there are two books, a black one and a white one. The white one is for the names of the people who helped save the Jews, the black one for the names of those who denounced and persecuted them. Two books representing two options: to save or to kill. Oskar Schindler or Amon Goeth. I don't like this simple division between good and evil.

Many Jews survived by going underground, thanks to help from relatives, friends, or work colleagues. These "quiet heroes" are not remembered often enough. Oskar Schindler was certainly not holier-than-thou but a rather ambiguous character. I find it hard to picture what he was really like.

■ ■ ■

Oskar Schindler and Amon Goeth: The two men were the same age and shared the same weakness for drink, parties, and women.

Both got rich on the back of the pogroms: Goeth by stealing from Jews and by killing them, by taking everything they had. Schindler by acquiring a factory in Krakow whose Jewish owners had been dispossessed and employing Jews from Goeth's camp as cheap labor.

Oskar Schindler, who had worked as an agent for the German counterintelligence in Poland, was a wartime profiteer at first; he came to Krakow to make a fortune. Later on he would spend most of the profits he had made on saving Jews.

The commandant Amon Goeth and the industrialist Oskar Schindler got on well together. Oskar Schindler needed cheap Jewish laborers and was therefore dependent on Amon Goeth's goodwill. Oskar Schindler called Goeth "Mony," brought him gifts, and introduced him to pretty women—among them Ruth Irene Kalder, who would eventually become Goeth's live-in lover.

Helen Rosenzweig, the Jewish maid in the Płaszów villa, reportedly said that Goeth believed that Schindler was his best friend. She, too, had been under that impression. True, Schindler had promised again and again to save her, "but then there he was again in his brown Nazi uniform taking part in Goeth's wild parties." There had been other factory owners who were helping Jewish workers and who depended on Goeth's goodwill. Yet they had not joined him in his revelries. "Schindler crossed limits that he didn't need to cross." Still, in the end she finds for Schindler: "Amon Goeth and Oskar Schindler, they both had power. One used it to kill, the other to save lives. Their example shows that everyone has a choice."

Steven Spielberg also plays with this motif in *Schindler's List*. He shows Amon Goeth as Schindler's evil twin. Both men appear to have been cut from the same wood, but their actions could not have been more different.

Goeth allowed Schindler to employ prisoners from the camp in his factory; he even allowed him to build an external camp for the workers at his factory where living conditions were much better than at Płaszów.

Amon Goeth's Jewish secretary Mietek Pemper and Oskar Schindler would sometimes hold secret meetings. Pemper said later that he had regarded Oskar Schindler as a savior from very early on. "No one other than Schindler was interested in our fate."

The Płaszów camp was run as a labor camp until the fall of 1943 when the SS administration decided to turn the last remaining labor camps into concentration camps. At the same time, more and more Polish camps which were not producing "strategic or pivotal" goods were being disbanded and the prisoners killed.

Consequently, Mietek Pemper conceived a plan: He wanted the Płaszów camp to be given the formal status of concentration camp because he was convinced that "the concentration camps will stay until the end of the war." Oskar Schindler claimed that apart from pots and pans his factory was also capable of making shell parts. Amon Goeth was just as keen on keeping "his" camp and presented his superiors with lists, manipulated by Mietek Pemper, of strategic goods produced at Płaszów. In fact, Płaszów officially operated as a concentration camp starting in January 1944. The prisoners were re-registered and were issued different clothes. New SS wardens arrived, and Amon Goeth was kept under tighter control. In his memoirs, Mietek Pemper explains that Goeth now needed written authorization from Berlin in order to torment his prisoners. He gives an example that highlights the bureaucracy of torture at the time: "A form had to be filled in with the requested number of lashes to the exposed buttocks." The camp's finances were also audited on a more regular basis now.

Amon Goeth had a look around other concentration camps and returned with new ideas, such as the tattooing of prisoners or the creation of a brothel for use by especially productive inmates. However, he never got a chance to implement these ideas.

By mid-1944 Płaszów was about to be disbanded. The Wehrmacht, the German army, was on the retreat, and the Red Army had entered Poland. In the summer of 1944, special SS task forces carried out a so-called "exhumation action" in Płaszów: All evidence of the exterminations was to be erased: The mass graves of the victims of the ghetto liquidation and other killings were dug up and the bodies burned. A putrid stench hung over the camp for weeks; the ashes were carried away by the truckload.

Emilie Schindler reported that in August 1944, her husband Oskar was worried about his laborers because Amon Goeth had decided to close Płaszów and send all the inmates to Auschwitz.

At the time, Oskar Schindler had his eye on an arms factory in Bruennlitz, near his hometown of Zwittau. His aim was to bring his workers there, to safety. Emilie Schindler described how her husband would bring Amon Goeth more and more expensive gifts. In the end, according to a number of different sources, the two men agreed upon a "deal": Amon Goeth would help Oskar Schindler smuggle "his" Jews to Bruennlitz, and Oskar Schindler would help Amon Goeth smuggle some of his valuable possessions to safety. Ultimately, however, Goeth's superiors in the SS also agreed to the transport of the "Schindler Jews" to Bruennlitz.

The list of people who were allowed to survive includes the names of around 800 men and 300 women. The circumstances behind each name's addition to the life-saving list are still unclear today. What is certain is that Marcel Goldberg, a Jewish camp inmate, took bribes and would swap names on the list for valuables.

After the war, Oskar Schindler did not meet with much success. Some of the Jews whose lives he had saved supported him financially. For his rescue of over 1,000 Jews, Schindler was named Righteous Among the Nations at a ceremony at the Israeli Holocaust memorial Yad Vashem in Jerusalem. He died in 1974 and was buried in Jerusalem.

There are many speculations as to what drove Schindler, what motives he had to save the Jews. Mietek Pemper sums Oskar Schindler up in these words: "This man, who had no special achievements to boast of, neither before the war nor after it, carried out a rescue operation, together with his wife, to which today, directly or indirectly, more than six

Oskar Schindler (2nd on the left) with some of his colleagues in Krakow, 1942

thousand people, including children and grandchildren, owe their lives. That is what's important. Nothing else matters."

■　■　■

OUR GUIDED TOUR OF THE MUSEUM has come to an end. I hang back to talk with the nice elderly lady from my group, the one who had offered me her umbrella. She is Jewish, from America, in her early seventies. She looks sporty, has short gray hair and bright eyes. I ask her if she has come to Krakow by herself. No, she replies, actually she's here with her husband. They are both Auschwitz survivors. Since they arrived in Poland, her husband has been gripped by a sudden fear, and he can't bring himself to revisit the scenes of his ordeal. He is distraught and stays in the hotel because he doesn't dare to go outdoors. That's why she went on her own— they had booked the tours before they came: Auschwitz yesterday, old Jewish Krakow today. She says it upsets her very much that her husband is suffering so much.

The story of the traumatized man who is too afraid to leave his hotel room moves me. I would like to cheer his wife up a little. I tell her that I have lived in Israel. She seems pleased and asks me what it was like for me there. We keep talking for a little while. She wants to know what I'm doing here, why I have come to Poland. Again I pretend that I am just a tourist with an interest in history. I offer her a lift in my taxi back toward Kazimierz, but she would rather walk a bit more.

For the second time today I have hidden my true identity. In the end I told Malgorzata, my tour guide, the whole story, but I couldn't tell it to this woman. I didn't want to tell her why I am here. There wouldn't have been enough time to explain everything. The knowledge would only have left her upset. She would have gone back to her husband in the hotel confused and maybe even troubled. But I am not comfortable with this secrecy either.

I will probably never see this friendly Jewish lady again, but sooner or later I will have to confide in my friends in Israel.

I head toward the Rynek, the magnificent medieval market square in the center of Krakow's Old Town. There is nothing gloomy about this place, there are no winding little alleys like in Kazimierz; here, everything is majestic and open. I browse the market stalls, looking for a bunch of flowers. I want something bright, but nothing gaudy. Mainly whites, with a mix of small and large flowers. I end up arranging my own.

■   ■   ■

During the German occupation, the Rynek in the center of Krakow was renamed Adolf Hitler Square. The Germans were already on the retreat

Amon Goeth (left) in Krakow on his way to court where he would be sentenced to death in September 1946

in Poland when the Płaszów commandant was arrested: The SS had discovered that Amon Goeth was secreting valuable assets away from Płaszów, so they initiated proceedings against their own man.

Goeth was accused of corruption and abuse of his position. He spent some time in Munich's Stadelheim prison but was soon released.

After a short stint at the front, Goeth was admitted to a hospital in the Bavarian town of Bad Toelz. His health had weakened; he was suffering from diabetes and had liver and kidney problems.

On April 30, 1945, the American army marched into Munich. On May 4, Amon Goeth—wearing only a Wehrmacht uniform and therefore not immediately identifiable as a member of the SS—was arrested in Bad Toelz. He gave a false name and claimed that he was a common soldier returning from the front. Meanwhile, his wife was filing for divorce in Vienna; she had heard of his affair with Ruth Irene Kalder.

The pregnant Kalder and her mother Agnes fled first to Vienna and then to Bad Toelz. On November 7, 1945, Goeth and Kalder's daughter, Monika, was born in Bad Toelz.

By then, Goeth had been taken to a detention camp on the grounds of the former Dachau concentration camp near Munich. From there, in January 1946, he wrote his last letter to Ruth Irene Kalder: "Dearest Ruth, Thank you for your letter and parcel. You poor thing, you have been through so much. . . . The food here is such that I only weigh 70kg now. It's enough. . . . Everything will be all right. Don't worry. . . . Lots of kisses for you and Monika and give my love to Omi. Love, Mony."

It wasn't long until the American investigators discovered who Goeth really was. Four former Płaszów prisoners identified him as the commandant of the camp. When they saw Amon Goeth in the company of American soldiers, one of the four witnesses greeted him with the words, "Herr Commandant, four Jewish pigs reporting for duty!"

Amon Goeth was extradited to Poland, together with the former commandant of the Auschwitz concentration camp, Rudolf Hoess. Goeth and Hoess arrived at Krakow's main station on July 30, 1946. An angry mob awaited them, but it wasn't Rudolf Hoess they were after, the man who had sent hundreds of thousands to their deaths in the gas chambers. It was Amon Goeth whom they wanted to lynch, the "Butcher of Płaszów."

Goeth was put on trial in Krakow in late August 1946. It was the first big trial of its kind in Poland, and it was going to last just a few days. The many spectators did not all fit into the courtroom, so the proceedings were broadcast to the outside via loudspeakers. Hundreds of listeners gathered on the lawns opposite the courthouse.

Goeth was charged with genocide. Among other crimes, he was accused of being responsible for the deaths of around 8,000 people at the Płaszów camp as well as the killings of 2,000 more during the liquidation of the Krakow ghetto. This was in addition to the murder of hundreds of people during the liquidation of the ghettos in Tarnow and Szebnie in the fall of 1943. Furthermore, he was charged with taking unlawful possession of the victims' valuables. Confronted with the number of witnesses for the prosecution, Amon Goeth reportedly called out: "What? So many Jews? And we were always told there'd be none left."

When Goeth was asked if he pleaded guilty, he retorted with a loud "No." At the trial he denied his crimes, giving the names of other SS men and saying that they had been responsible for the killings. He had only been following orders, he said, he had been a common soldier and had not given any orders himself. When witnesses described the murders in the camp, he looked away indifferently or tried to prove that they were making false claims. He called Oskar Schindler as a witness for the defense, but he did not turn up.

Absurdly, he also called his former secretary Mietek Pemper as a witness, but Pemper, who had witnessed many of Goeth's crimes, spoke against him rather than for him.

The Polish prosecutor demanded the death penalty and said in his summation to the jury: "You are being asked to judge a man who has become a legend during his lifetime for being the modern incarnation of the biblical Satan."

Amon Goeth was indeed sentenced to death. He appealed for clemency and asked for the death penalty to be changed into a prison sentence. He wanted to prove that he could be a useful member of society. The appeal was denied.

On September 13, 1946, Amon Goeth was led to the gallows. His last words were "Heil Hitler."

■　■　■

THERE ARE MANY THINGS I'd like to ask my grandmother. I think it would have been worthwhile to press her for answers—she had some dents in her armor and might have been willing to talk.

As for my grandfather, I have few questions for him. Those images of his execution, of his arm raised defiantly in the air, the Hitler salute his parting gesture from life. If he had ever shown any signs of remorse, I would have liked to question him. Yet, as it was, I think it would have been pointless. He never admitted his guilt. At his trial he lied right up to the end.

I go to visit the former site of the Płaszów concentration camp.

Today the hilly ground where the camp used to be is turfed over. There is nothing here to recall the barbed-wire fences, the watchtowers, the quarry where the prisoners toiled, the barracks, the mass graves. Only green grass, in between a McDonald's restaurant and a busy highway. In the distance, socialist prefab buildings loom against the sky.

High on a hill, visible from afar, stands the memorial: a larger-than-life sculpture of people with bowed heads, carved from light-colored stone. Where their hearts should be is a gaping hole.

I am surprised. I can still picture this setting from *Schindler's List*. Everything seemed so real, so alive. Now there are no moving pictures, only stones.

The camp is history; my grandfather has long been dead.

I hold onto my flowers and climb the wide steps up to the plateau where the memorial stands. From up here I get a much better view of the area. The site looks abandoned and neglected. Without the informational displays, one would never guess at the atrocities that were committed here all those years ago.

People are jogging by in the drizzling rain; in the distance I can make out others walking their dogs. They probably come here every day, grateful for this park's existence.

All alone I stand in front of the memorial. Few people come here at this time of year.

The memorial for the victims of the Płaszów camp

Reverently, I touch the cold stone with my hand, just like I did at the Wailing Wall in Jerusalem.

During the last few months I've been asking myself, *Who am I?* I'm not so sure anymore: Am I still Jennifer, or am I only Jennifer, the granddaughter of Amon Goeth, now? What counts in my life?

I can't just shove my grandfather's past into a box and put a lid on it. I can't just say, *That's the past, it's over, it doesn't affect me anymore.* That would be a betrayal of the victims.

I have come here as I would come to a grave. A grave is a place to care for and to return to in order to honor the dead.

When somebody dies it is not necessarily essential to go to their funeral. You can say good-bye privately. Yet the visit to the grave is a sign, an important ritual, which is why I have come here today. I want to pay my respects to the victims. To show that I will never forget them.

Slowly I lay down the flowers and sit on the grass. Only now do I realize that a group of people has gathered in front of the memorial. Children are running over the grass. A school class from Israel. I listen; it sounds dear and familiar.

CHAPTER 3

THE COMMANDANT'S MISTRESS:

MY GRANDMOTHER RUTH IRENE KALDER

It was a wonderful time. My Amon was king, I was his queen.
Who wouldn't have relished that?
—RUTH IRENE GOETH IN 1975,
about her time spent with concentration camp commandant Amon Goeth

OW MUCH DID MY GRANDMOTHER KNOW?
Before my visit to the villa I had convinced myself that
she probably wasn't aware of everything that was going on.

Before going to Krakow I had imagined rambling grounds, a massive house. The shots fired in the camp would have been too far away, the screams of the maids being terrorized by my grandfather too quiet to hear.

Only it wasn't like that. My grandmother was right in the thick of it. The house was small, the camp not far away.

Was my grandmother not just blinded by love but deafened by it, too?

Where was my grandmother's compassion? People were dying a few hundred yards away, and there she was, reveling with Amon Goeth.

My grandfather has long been dead, but I knew my grandmother. When I was a small child, she was the person who mattered most to me. I had little, if anything, to hold on to. She liked me, and that meant a lot.

To me, she radiated kindness. Whenever I think of her, I feel safe and secure again.

And then I read the book about my mother, and now I am learning all these things about my grandmother that blatantly contradict the image I have of her.

If it hadn't been for her, maybe discovering Amon Goeth in my family tree wouldn't have been such a shock. I could have regarded him more as a historical figure; I might not have taken it quite so personally. Yes, he is my grandfather, but he never pushed my stroller or held my hand. But my grandmother did.

I feel so close to her, which is why I cannot simply shove the image of Amon Goeth to some distant place in history.

Literature written about the descendants of Nazi criminals sometimes differentiates between those who knew the relative in question and those who didn't. Some authors conclude that those who never met their Nazi ancestor are generally less troubled by their past. What they ignore, however, is that those born after the event often still know relatives who loved their Nazi ancestor. The living are their connection to the dead.

My mother was ten months old, a baby, when Amon Goeth was executed. Yet the book about her clearly shows that she is very distressed by the past. She has the same connection to him as I do: Ruth Irene—her mother, my grandmother. The woman who had a picture of Amon Goeth hanging above her bed until her death. My grandmother later said that he was the most important man in her life. What drew her to him?

The large bus I am on is full of people, but nobody is talking much. We drive along roads lined with low houses; the route is dotted with little villages. The pavement is wet. It has been raining again. I wish the sun would break through the clouds—the place where I'm heading is gloomy enough as it is.

It is my second and last day in Poland, and I am on my way to

Auschwitz. The former concentration camp is only an hour's drive away from Krakow. I have never been there before, even though Auschwitz is both a powerful symbol and harrowing relic of the Holocaust. Visiting these places is an altogether different experience from just reading about them. Auschwitz is where Amon Goeth sent thousands of Płaszów prisoners—straight to the gas chambers. Did he talk to my grandmother about it? Maybe not, but she must have known it nonetheless.

The more I try to understand who she really was, the harder I find it to stay objective.

■　■　■

Jennifer Teege's grandmother Ruth Irene Kalder, later Ruth Irene Goeth, was 25 years old when she met Amon Goeth. She came from Gleiwitz in Upper Silesia. Her father owned a driving school and was a member of the Nazi party. Ruth Irene Kalder had qualified as a beautician and had attended a drama school in Essen. During her time there, she allegedly had a relationship with an older man, got pregnant, and subsequently had an abortion.

In Krakow she was working as a secretary for the Wehrmacht. According to Goeth's biographer Johannes Sachslehner, she "had a reputation for not being disinclined to little adventures with men in uniform." She became friendly with the industrialist Oskar Schindler and carried out some secretarial jobs for him. One evening in the spring of 1943, Schindler took her along to a dinner with Amon Goeth.

Later, in interviews and when talking to her daughter Monika, Ruth Irene Kalder described meeting the concentration camp commandant as love at first sight. Amon Goeth was big and strong, she said, "a true dream for any secretary." She had "eyes for nobody but this man," adding that he was funny, intelligent, and well read, "the ideal man, like Clark Gable as Rhett Butler in *Gone with the Wind*."

In an interview with the Israeli historian and journalist Tom Segev in 1975, Ruth Irene Kalder also claimed that she was supposed to flirt with Amon Goeth in order to cement his good relationship with Oskar Schindler, who relied on Jewish laborers sourced from Goeth's camp. "My job as the pretty secretary was to win over his heart so that he would continue to provide us with these workers, since the Jews were now under the control of the camp commandant."

The petite, dark-haired young woman instantly hit it off with Amon Goeth. Ruth Irene Kalder recalled that they were soon on first-name terms; as she was leaving, Goeth said to her, "I'll call you." When he hadn't been in touch after a few days, she called him: "You said you'd call, I'm still waiting." Goeth was surprised but also suspicious. He was under the impression that she was Oskar Schindler's girlfriend and had called to spy on him. She reassured him that she was only friends with Schindler and arranged to meet him in Płaszów.

She soon became Goeth's permanent girlfriend; he gave her the pet name *Majola*. Her love for Amon Goeth brought her to the grounds of a concentration camp, into the house of its commandant.

Goeth's former Jewish maid Helen Rosenzweig has described Ruth Irene Kalder as a "beautiful young woman, with dark hair and wonderfully milky skin. She must have been very much in love with Goeth, for she was always gazing at him."

Kalder ignored her beloved Amon's less loveable side. According to Helen Rosenzweig, Ruth Irene Kalder did not want to know what was going on in the camp: "Most of the time she was busy mixing egg yolk with cucumber and yogurt, and then she would lie around with a cucumber mask on her face. She would turn the music way up so that she couldn't hear the shots."

Film director Steven Spielberg shows Ruth Irene Kalder burying her head in her pillow while Amon Goeth is shooting from his balcony.

Ruth Irene's mother, Agnes Kalder, visited her daughter at Płaszów once. Agnes was horrified to see the environment where her daughter was living and returned home early.

Ruth Irene Kalder, however, enjoyed her life of luxury at the commandant's side. She later told her daughter Monika that she and Goeth would often start the day with a horseback ride. Afterward, she would apply her extensive makeup. After breakfast she would give the orders for lunch: plenty of meat and alcohol for Amon Goeth, cake and fruit for dessert. In the afternoons, Ruth Irene Kalder would go for another ride, listen to

Ruth Irene Kalder, photographed by Amon Goeth, with Rolf, the Great Dane that Goeth trained to tear humans apart, and her own lapdog

music, or play tennis with the girlfriends and wives of the other SS men. In the evenings there would often be company. Amon Goeth and his girlfriend especially enjoyed having the Rosner brothers, Jewish musicians from the camp, perform for them. On those occasions, Hermann and Poldek Rosner would swap their prison clothes for elegant suits and play the violin and the accordion for Goeth and his guests. And Ruth Irene Kalder, dressed in fine clothes from Krakow shops, would play the lady of the house.

One photo from Płaszów shows Ruth Irene posing in an elegant riding dress in front of the somber barracks and barbed-wire fences as if she were modeling the latest fashion on the Champs-Élysées. In other photos she is sunbathing in a swimsuit on the patio of the commandant's villa. Another picture shows her in a stylish hat and coat, standing with her little black lapdog on one side and Goeth's favorite dog, his spotted Great Dane Rolf, on the other. Presumably, Amon Goeth took this picture of her.

■   ■   ■

FOR ALL THESE YEARS, I've had only one photograph of my grandmother. It shows her wearing a long, flowery dress, her hair combed into a beehive, the golden bangle on her arm twinkling in the sun. She is standing on the grass in the English Garden in Munich. A dachshund is playing behind her, a red ball lying in the grass. She is smiling at the camera and looks young, happy, and relaxed. It is a lovely, natural photo, which I have always treasured.

Now I am finding very different pictures of her, in the book about my mother and on the Internet. Looking at these pictures of her, posing with a dog that would attack people on Goeth's command—it is unbearable; it is too upsetting. I am exposing myself to a lot, but I can't and won't look at these pictures. How could she touch this dog, how could she bear having it near her? After all, it wasn't a pet, but an animal trained to kill.

I cannot reconcile these pictures with my image of her.

I do not grieve for my grandfather, but I do for my grandmother. I grieve for the person she never really was.

She was always good to me, which is why I always thought of her as a good person. As a child, you cannot imagine that the person you love could have another side, a darker one.

I really wish that my memories of her had not been tarnished. Why couldn't she have been just an ordinary grandmother—a nice lady who died one day?

I had always thought of Irene as one of my three grandmothers, the other two being my adoptive grandmothers, whom I called *Oma Vienna* and *Oma Bochum*.

Oma Bochum was my adoptive father's mother. She was very short, had gray curly hair—a typical grandmother's perm—and an energetic, scurrying walk. She would always wear skirts, covered with an apron to keep them clean. Whenever she left the house she would change into her orthopedic pumps with flat heels—the ones I called "click-clack shoes" as a child. When I went to visit her in Bochum with my adoptive family, we would accompany her to the market or to the butcher's, or help with her gardening. I was never too enthusiastic about planting vegetables or picking fruit, but I loved the results: The shelves in her basement were loaded with jars of stewed fruit. At dinnertime, a gong would summon us to the table.

She was very disciplined and also a little strict, not a cuddly grandmother. Yet she had a big heart. Even though my Oma Bochum had two children of her own—my adoptive father and his sister—she regarded it her Christian duty to include other children in her family. Helping orphaned or neglected children was a living family tradition. Growing up with a number of foster siblings was a matter of course for my adoptive father, which is why it later seemed natural to him to take in a foster child—me.

My Oma Bochum was an active member of the Protestant Church and very popular in the community. She would regularly visit the grave of her late husband, who had died young. She normally went to church on Sundays, and eventually she died there, too: She had a heart attack one Sunday in the middle of a service.

My Oma Vienna, my adoptive mother's mother, was also short, but very plump. She exuded something motherly, calming. She was always impeccably dressed and enjoyed wearing silk dresses and fur-trimmed coats. As a child, I often stayed with her; I preferred Vienna to Bochum—the city was more exciting. Oma Vienna would sometimes behave like a small child herself: Once we played a trick on Opa and pretended that we had all run away, Oma and the children. Opa played along, pretending to be really worried.

Only Christmastime was odd with Oma Vienna. We would all sing carols under the tree, but she wouldn't join in for fear of striking the wrong notes.

We often went on vacation with our grandparents from Vienna, too: skiing in the winter, hiking in the Austrian Alps, or camping by the sea in Italy in the summer. Opa sometimes told us wartime stories about his time with Rommel in Africa. Oma never talked to us about the war. In 1945, she had fled the area that is now the Czech Republic for Vienna. The journey was a terrible experience for her, but she would never discuss it.

And then there is my fourth grandmother, in Nigeria—my other biological grandmother besides Irene. I don't know much about her. I met my father once, when I was 28. He told me that, when my mother wanted to give me away to the orphanage, he had suggested that I might as well live with his mother in Nigeria. He would have preferred that to the orphanage, but my mother didn't like the idea. I guess she wasn't ready then to give me up entirely. While I was at the orphanage, my mother could still visit me, and she would still have had the option to take me back.

I imagine my African grandmother as a tall, proud woman, a strict matriarch. I find it remarkable that she would have been prepared to take me in. For that I am very grateful to her, and I sometimes wonder, what if . . . ?

I have never compared my grandmothers to each other, during my childhood or later. They were far too dissimilar for that. I had separate relationships with each of them, and each was important in her own way.

Nonetheless, Irene occupied a special place in my heart. She was one of the first people I was attached to as a child.

When I was seven and my adoption became official, my adoptive parents broke off all contact with my mother; they thought that it would be best for me. With that, my grandmother also disappeared from my life. She left behind a gap, I missed her.

I was 13 when last I heard about her: My adoptive parents told me that my grandmother had died. They had seen the obituary notice in the newspaper. It didn't mention that she had killed herself.

I didn't ask any questions. My biological family was not a subject we talked about in my new family. There was a deep and stony silence—a tacit agreement between my adoptive parents and me not to mention my mother or grandmother. Not that my adoptive parents could have told me much about them anyway; they didn't know anything.

I remember feeling sad when I heard about my grandmother's death. I had always hoped to see her again one day, but now she was gone for good.

Before I came across the book in the library, all I had were my memories: My grandmother enjoyed my company. With my mother I often felt that I wasn't welcome—my mother would pull me along by the arm when she was impatient, but Irene never did.

I remember only one exchange with my grandmother that confused me: For some reason I was feeling sad, but she was very unsympathetic and told me not to cry. I didn't understand what my grandmother had against tears.

She was not your classic grandmother; I wasn't even allowed to call her *Oma*, just Irene. Maybe she didn't want to be considered old. It's been said that she paid a lot of attention to her looks—her appearance was very important to her. Even my mother called her only by her first name; that's what it says in the book.

I remember her apartment in Schwind Strasse, in Schwabing. We would usually sit in her open-plan kitchen with the American radio station AFN turned on. I still enjoy listening to English-language radio stations; in Hamburg I often tuned into a British military station, and in Israel I'd listen to the Voice of Peace.

She didn't have a living room, as such. At home with my adoptive family in the Waldtrudering suburb of Munich, we would hang out on the sofa in the living room, and we would wear comfortable "house clothes" indoors. This would have been unthinkable at Irene's. It is true that I always felt at ease with my grandmother, but never quite at home: I was still a visitor. She was always elegantly dressed and nicely made up—everything was a little formal. The kitchen was always clean and tidy; I never saw her cooking or baking.

Unfortunately I have far too few concrete memories of her; I think of her as a child would: someone who cares, someone who protects.

Whenever my mother picked me up from the orphanage—or later, from my foster family—and dropped me off at my grandmother's, it meant that I didn't have to go my mother's place in Hasenbergl.

It wasn't like my mother had a happy family at home: Her then-husband was a drunkard and a wife-beater, and I felt constantly threatened by him. I never knew whether he was going to be there or not. If he was out, I'd hope that he wouldn't come back. I was always listening for the sound of his key in the lock or his footsteps in the corridor.

At my grandmother's, I felt safe. When I entered her kitchen, everything was all right.

◼ ◼ ◼

Helen Rosenzweig, Goeth's former Jewish maid, tells this story about Ruth Irene Kalder: "Once she came down to see us in the kitchen. She reached out her hands to us and said: 'If I could send you home I would, but it's not in my power.'"

In Amon Goeth's villa, the maids, Helen Hirsch and Helen Rosenzweig, were subjected to constant abuse: He summoned them by shouting or by ringing a bell that could be heard all over the house. Often he would beat them if they didn't come running fast enough. One of those beatings left Helen Hirsch with a burst left eardrum; she remained deaf in that ear. Helen Rosenzweig has described how Goeth pushed her down the stairs countless times. "In his house, at his mercy, I lost all fear of death. It was like living under the gallows, twenty-four hours a day."

Ruth Irene Kalder later told her daughter Monika that she once intervened when Goeth was threatening to beat one of the maids with a bull pizzle—a dried bull's penis that was used as a flogging tool in the concentration camps. In the ensuing struggle, Amon ended up hitting Ruth, which he felt awful about. He came close to tears, she said, and apologized over and over, and after that he never again used a bull pizzle in the house. Ruth Irene also told her daughter another grotesque anecdote: She once threatened not to sleep with Goeth anymore "if he didn't stop shooting at the Jews." Apparently it worked.

Helen Rosenzweig felt she had spotted a "shred of humanity" in Ruth Irene Kalder. She remembers, for example, that Ruth would make it a point to praise the maids in front of Amon Goeth and that she always treated them with respect.

When Helen Rosenzweig's sisters were to be transported from Płaszów—presumably to Auschwitz—Helen Hirsch ran to Ruth Irene Kalder and begged her to prevent their deportation. At first, she refused: "Please don't ask me to do this!" Eventually, however, she caved in and called the camp police to stop the deportation of the Rosenzweig sisters. When Ruth Irene confessed her unauthorized rescue mission to Goeth, he was furious. According to Helen Hirsch, he came running to the kitchen with his rifle to find the maids, but eventually he calmed down.

Helen Hirsch also reported that the inebriated Goeth once tried to sexually assault her. Ruth Irene Kalder heard her cries and came running to her rescue. Goeth then let her go.

There are a number of eyewitnesses who remember that Ruth Irene Kalder tried to exert a moderating influence on Amon Goeth's behavior. She is said to have taken a stand for individual prisoners and to have prevented the torture and shooting of a number of inmates. In her presence, Amon Goeth is said to have been more restrained and mild-mannered. In another example, according to contemporary witnesses, she once called Goeth away from the parade ground while he was having prisoners whipped. Ruth Irene Kalder, however, would later claim that she never set foot in the camp.

Emilie Schindler recounted that around the middle of 1944, her husband Oskar reported that Goeth was getting tired of his girlfriend; the woman was "too peace-loving" and always trying "to dissuade him from his sadistic excesses."

That said, the fact that Ruth Irene Kalder sometimes half-heartedly tried to help the victims goes to show that she knew how Amon Goeth was treating them and what crimes were being committed in the camp.

In his autobiography, Goeth's secretary Mietek Pemper writes that Ruth Irene Kalder would sometimes type highly confidential documents for Goeth. Pemper believes that she also helped compile a list of prisoners to be executed.

Later, Ruth Irene Kalder would often stress two things, namely that Płaszów had only ever been a labor camp, not a death camp, and that there had been only adults in the camp, and no children.

Nonetheless, she told her daughter Monika that she had once observed children being transported from the camp by truck. Monika Goeth has said that her mother could not stop thinking about those children and that she believes her mother put her memories of the event to paper.

The trucks Ruth Irene Kalder remembered were probably those which took the children from Płaszów to Auschwitz on May 14, 1944. Goeth needed to create space in his camp for a number of Hungarian Jews who were due to arrive. Accordingly, he wrote in a letter to an SS leader, he had to "purge" the camp of its old, ill, and weak inmates, as well as its children, and thereby liquidate all the "unproductive elements." In other words, he was going to deport the weak and the ill from Płaszów to the gas chambers at the nearby camp of Auschwitz, for "special treatment."

Notices were put up at the parade ground proclaiming "Appropriate work for every prisoner." Loudspeakers blared out cheery tunes as the prisoners were told to undress and parade past the camp doctors. According to an eyewitness, among them was Josef Mengele, the infamous camp doctor from Auschwitz, who had come specially and was noting down the names of the children. A week later, the result of this so-called "health action" was announced. Those who were to be removed to Auschwitz had to gather on one side of the square: around 1,200 people in total, including about 250 children.

Płaszów survivor Stella Mueller-Madej describes the scene as the children were being herded onto the truck: "The whole place is pandemonium. Fathers and mothers are sobbing. The children, who until then had been silent like dolls and frozen with horror, are now screaming and pleading . . . They are crying for help . . . A very young child tries to crawl away to safety on all fours. A female guard . . . grabs . . . her by her hands and throws her little body onto the truck bed like a sack of potatoes. It is unbearable. Everyone on the parade ground is crying, the whips are lashing down, the dogs are barking . . . At that moment the loudspeakers start to play waltz music . . . and the trucks head off to the camp gate."

Shortly after their arrival at Auschwitz, the children were killed.

◾ ◾ ◾

JUST AS MY GRANDMOTHER, HER WHOLE LIFE, made excuses for Amon Goeth and romanticized him, I tended to regard her too favorably in the beginning of my research. I told myself, "She didn't do anyone any harm. She was not actively involved in his deeds."

I knew so little about my grandmother. I saw my mother once again in my early twenties, but my grandmother had already passed away by then. When reading the book about my mother, I scrutinized the pictures of Irene closely—at first only the private ones from the years after the war, and then later the historic ones, too. Sometimes I can see myself in her.

I also love the good life. I drive a comfortable car, enjoy living in a big house, and appreciate modern conveniences. Like my grandmother, I like beautiful things, and I don't mind if they cost a little extra. But surely the question is: How high is the price?

I don't think it was just the status and the money that kept my grandmother in Płaszów—she undeniably enjoyed living in prosperity with Goeth, but I doubt that the luxury lifestyle alone would have been enough. After the war, she lived a much more modest life.

I think she was madly in love with Amon Goeth. Maybe she was also fascinated by his power, but there must have been more, some sort of inescapable pull or need, which blocked out everything else.

My grandmother never married or had a long-term relationship later in life. No matter who drifted in or out of her life after the war, Amon's photograph always hung in the same spot—another reason I think her relationship with Amon Goeth was based on more than a mere cost-benefit calculation.

I know how this feels, this evidently boundless love, because I'm exactly the same way. When I love someone, I love unconditionally. In this I can understand my grandmother. When I'm in love with a man, I give him carte blanche: In theory, he can do as he likes; he will always have a special place in my heart. I won't tell him so, of course, and it doesn't mean that I will always tolerate or approve of his behavior, but the love will always be there.

That raises the question, what would I have done in my grandmother's place? Could I have fallen for this sadist of a man? I can't give a straight answer to that, but just the thought of someone beating his servants with a bull pizzle is enough to turn my stomach.

By way of apology for my grandmother, my mother has said that the camp was not visible from the bedroom at the villa. The Jews in the camp allegedly said of my grandmother: "She's one of us." Her name was Ruth, after all, a Jewish name.

Am I to believe that? Or am I just glad to have an excuse? I am of two minds: On the one hand, I want to sustain the lovely image of my grandmother. On the other hand, I want to know the truth. At college I used to gather reference material and compare the different sources. What mattered in the end were not my assumptions, but the hard facts. It is the same with my grandmother: I have gathered a lot of material about her in order to gain a better understanding of her.

I am no judge; it is not my place to pass judgment on her. I just want to see her as who she really was.

My first reaction when I read about her trying to help the victims was one of relief. I thought, "She wasn't like my grandfather, maybe she was on the side of good." But now I am ashamed of this thought.

I try to picture the scene with the maids again: My grandmother standing in the kitchen and telling Helen, who had to fear for her life every moment of every day, that she would help her if only she could. There is a great coldness in that, too. She took a step toward Helen, but then abandoned her after all.

She had seen the maids' suffering; she was aware that she was caught in a predicament. But that's the fatal thing: She could tell right from wrong. She could have made a choice. But she was too selfish to let this inner conflict come to the surface.

She felt pity for others and even helped some of them. But is that enough? Absolutely not. I don't care whether she intervened a hundred times or a thousand. The fact is, it didn't change her priorities. In the end, she was just looking out for herself.

I believe that there is a difference between me and my grandmother, and a very fundamental one: I could never live with a murderer; I could never bear to be with a man who took pleasure in tormenting other people.

■　■　■

Whenever Jennifer Teege talks about her grandmother, her voice goes soft and her eyes beam.

Her feelings fluctuate between rejection and affection, attack and defense. She cannot get a handle on who her grandmother really was.

"I had no idea." Ruth Irene Kalder would repeat this sentence often after the war. It is a sentence that many young Germans have grown up with: Parents and grandparents claim they had no knowledge of the murder of countless people—and their children and grandchildren don't know whether or not to believe them, whether or not they *should* believe them.

But surely you must have known!

Is it possible that no knowledge of what was really going on filtered down to the ordinary Germans?

In 2011, Friedrich Kellner's diaries from the years 1939 to 1945 were published for the first time. During the war, Friedrich Kellner was a simple judicial officer. He came from a modest background and lived in the Hessian backcountry until his death in 1970. He had no access to secret files, but simply wrote down the bits of information he overheard, gleaned from conversation with other locals and, above all, read in newspapers available to the general public. His diaries are evidence of what those who "had no idea" could have known about the dictatorial regime, the war, and the Holocaust. For example, in 1941 Friedrich Kellner wrote: "The mental asylums have turned into centers for murder." Reading the newspapers, he had noticed a suspiciously high number of death notices for people in mental hospitals. He had also been told about a case where a couple was able to bring their mentally ill son home from such a hospital just in time. Around the same time, immediately after the attack on the Soviet Union, Friedrich Kellner heard about the mass murder of the Jews: "A soldier who was home on leave described the awful atrocities he had witnessed in occupied Poland. He had seen how naked Jews, men and women, were made to stand in front of a long, deep trench. Upon SS command, a number of Ukrainian men shot them in the backs of their heads and they fell into the trench. The trenches were filled in even though screams could still be heard from within!" In September 1942, two Jewish families were deported from Kellner's hometown, Laubach. In his diary he writes: "In the last few days, the Jews from our district have been deported. From Laubach they took the Strausses and the Heinemanns. A well-informed source tells me that all the Jews are being taken to Poland, where they will be murdered by SS troops."

In 1996, the artist Gunter Demnig started laying *stolpersteine*, or "stumbling blocks"—cobblestone-sized, brass memorials—in front of houses where victims of the Nazis used to live. Now in over 800 German towns and villages, they make the number of victims palpable: In some streets there are *stolpersteine* in front of every other house, sometimes with a single name, sometimes with the names of an entire family. On these streets it would have been glaringly obvious that some neighbors were missing: the Jewish family, the girl with Down syndrome, the homosexual, the communist.

Yet in many German families, the parents and grandparents have never been asked any probing questions. "The Nazis" were others. It is inconceivable that the friendly grandfather might have committed any crimes on the frontline, or that the kindly grandmother might have cheered Hitler. Just as unimaginable as it was for Jennifer Teege to discover that her grandmother once enjoyed the good life on the edge of a concentration camp.

This self-delusion, this schizophrenic view of one's own historical narrative, is rarely as apparent as it is with Ruth Irene Kalder. She was no perpetrator, but she was a bystander and a profiteer. Amon Goeth made his career, and she joined him in it. Amon Goeth remains a stranger we can distance ourselves from, but in Ruth Irene Kalder, the seduced opportunist, we can recognize some part of ourselves.

When she learned of Amon Goeth's execution from the newsreel, Ruth Irene Kalder is said to have ranted and raved. Monika Goeth remembers her grandmother, Agnes Kalder, claiming that Ruth Irene's hair went white and that she subsequently died it black.

Monika Goeth also recounts that her mother repeatedly watched the American film *I Want to Live* with Susan Hayward in the title role. The film makes a passionate plea against the death penalty; it shows an innocent woman being executed for a murder she didn't commit.

The Third Man was also among her favorite films. Ruth Irene Kalder is said to have seen herself in the beautiful actress Alida Valli. In the famous post-war film, Alida Valli plays the girlfriend of murderer Harry Lime, played by Orson Welles. She stands by her lover with total devotion, loyal to the grave.

According to her daughter Monika, Ruth Irene Kalder did go on to have relationships with other men, but she didn't love any of them as she had loved Amon. After the war, she dated a US army officer for a short while. He paid for her English lessons. Even after he returned home to his wife and child in Texas, he continued to send her regular love letters and monthly checks until her suicide in 1983.

In 1948, two years after Amon Goeth's execution, Ruth Irene Kalder asked the American authorities in US-occupied Germany to allow her to take on Goeth's name, claiming that it was only the confusion at the end of the war that had prevented them from getting married.

Goeth's father, Amon Franz Goeth, with whom Kalder had been corresponding, supported her request. He confirmed that his son and Ruth Irene Kalder had gotten engaged before the end of the war. Since Goeth's divorce from his second wife had already been finalized, Ruth Irene was allowed to drop her maiden name, Kalder. From then on she was known as Ruth Irene Goeth.

Amon Goeth lived on in her stories—as a charming, witty gentleman from Vienna who sadly died a hero's death in the war. Ruth Irene Goeth never spoke of the crimes committed during the war; in this she was no different from most of her contemporaries. More than once, Ruth Irene struck her daughter Monika because she would not stop asking questions.

Monika Goeth describes her mother as self-absorbed and cold-hearted, a woman who was mainly concerned with her own beauty. When she had a facelift, she also had her nose, which she considered "Jewish-looking," straightened. She was a woman who carried a lifelong unhappiness because the world had taken her great love away from her too soon.

It does not appear as if Ruth Irene secreted away any of the riches Amon Goeth had amassed in Płaszów. Ruth Irene Kalder worked as a secretary and sometimes posed as a fashion model for catalogues; in the evenings she often worked at the *Gruene Gans*—the Green Goose, a bar in the trendy quarter of Schwabing. Her daughter Monika has described how her mother loved strutting around Schwabing in a dress to match her lipstick, with her equally well-groomed poodle, Monsieur, by her side.

Ruth Irene was not interested in Monika or her problems, Monika Goeth has said of her mother: "Ruth wasn't concerned with much. What feelings she had were reserved for her dead lover, for Amon."

THE BOOK ABOUT MY MOTHER DELIVERS a double blow: It broke my enchantment with my grandmother twice. She is described as heartless and selfish: first at the side of the concentration camp commandant, and then as a terrible mother. Even worse than that—as a monstrous kind of mother who neglects and hits her daughter. In the book, my mother criticizes her severely; she hardly has anything kind to say about her at all.

I don't think that is very fair to my grandmother. After all, she is dead and can't defend herself.

At the same time, the book clearly illustrates the degree to which my mother's life has been dominated by her struggle with my grandmother. But despite everything, they always kept in touch. When my mother was pregnant with me, she even lived with Irene for a while.

What is striking is the close relationship my mother had with her grandmother Agnes, Irene's mother. My mother spent her entire childhood living with her mother and grandmother in the apartment in Schwabing. A household with three women, three generations beneath one roof. The men—my great-grandfather and Amon Goeth—were dead.

According to the book, my grandmother was jealous of Monika's close relationship with Agnes; she felt like an outsider between two soulmates. During my mother's childhood, Agnes was her calm anchor and her pillar of support.

Sometimes I feel like history is repeating itself: Just as my mother had a close relationship with her grandmother and a difficult one with her mother, I used to feel at home with my grandmother and uncomfortable with my own mother. It appears that love tends to skip a generation in my family.

Again and again my mother stresses how obsessed my grandmother was with her looks, and how beautiful she was—like a young Elizabeth Taylor. While Irene was always dressed smartly, Monika allegedly ran around in rags.

Irene is reduced to her failures as a mother, and to her vanity—as if she had spent half her life in front of the mirror perfecting her makeup.

I don't believe that Irene was only selfish and vain. She was an attractive and unusual woman. She didn't look for a provider, which was the norm in postwar Germany, but stood on her own two feet: She worked as a secretary at the Goethe Institute for many years. This is something else we have in common: I also worked at the Goethe Institute, while studying in Israel.

What was unusual for somebody of her generation was that she spoke very good English and often read the British *Times*. Her apartment was full of books, among them Tucholsky, Boell, and Brecht. She was interested in drama and literature. She voted for the socialist SPD party and was a fan of the politician Willy Brandt.

My grandmother was very liberal for her time: For a while she shared her flat with a transvestite called Lulu and went out on the town with him and his gay friends. My parents met when one of my father's friends, also African, was living as a lodger in my grandmother's house. Having an African man living in your house was far from normal in Munich in the 1960s and '70s. She was no racist.

I would have loved to ask my grandmother's friends some questions about her, but all I have is what journalists have reported about her—and my mother's opinions. Neither source is exactly full of praise. Usually I can trust my gut; I have a keen sense of character. Can I really have been so wrong about my grandmother?

When I was about seventeen years old, my adoptive parents gave me a postcard from my grandmother. They had kept it from me until then because they were worried that I would be torn between my old family and my new one. My grandmother had sent me the card for my seventh birthday, together with a picture book she had picked out for me. I would have preferred to have received these things much earlier. It would have been helpful and important to me—after all, they were tangible possessions, memories of the natural family who had suddenly disappeared from my life when I was adopted.

My grandmother's postcard is of a painting by Paula Modersohn-Becker, *Peasant Girl with Arms Folded.* It shows a serious and

Paula Modersohn-Becker's painting Peasant Girl with Arms Folded. *Ruth Irene Goeth sent this card to her granddaughter for Jennifer's seventh birthday*

proud-looking young girl, her arms crossed in front of her body. She is about the same age I would have been when my grand-mother wrote the card. Irene's handwriting is itself a work of art. She took great care in writing the card, care that is typical of her generation. She wrote, "Dear Jennifer, wishing you a wonderful birthday and another 364 happy days in your new year. Do you like reading? I hope so, and if you do I am sure you will enjoy this book. I think of you often. Give my regards to your parents. Yours, Irene." The message is lovely and heartfelt. It makes me happy to see the word "Yours" in front of her signature.

■ ■ ■

Inge Sieber, Jennifer Teege's adoptive mother, remembers that for a while, when she was still small, Jennifer hoped that her grandmother would take her in.

Once, before the adoption, Ruth Irene Goeth visited Jennifer and her new family. She called beforehand and asked if she could come by, so Jennifer's foster parents invited her for afternoon coffee. Inge Sieber found Ruth Irene to be friendly and thoughtful; she was wearing a long patchwork skirt and looked nothing like a grandma. "She was dressed in these shabby-chic clothes. Flashy, extravagant, but not false. I was 25 years younger, but next to her I felt like a little old housewife." Jennifer's grandmother stayed for a couple of hours, asked lots of questions, and was generally very interested in Jennifer's new family.

At around the same time, in the mid-'70s, the Israeli historian Tom Segev visited Ruth Irene Goeth at her apartment in Schwabing.

Segev was not yet the scientist and journalist of international fame he would go on to become; he was just a young PhD student from Boston University. For his thesis on concentration camp commandants, he traveled all over Germany to interview the close relatives and friends of many Nazi perpetrators. He hoped that they would provide answers to his questions about the camp commandants' frame of mind and the motives that drove them. His work was published under the title *Soldiers of Evil: The Commandants of the Nazi Concentration Camps.*

His study sheds light on not only the commandants' psyche, but also that of their closest relatives, usually their widows. Segev writes: "They agree to be interviewed by me because they are haunted by a past that they cannot seem to escape. . . . Each of these people hoped that they could whitewash their past, if only a little bit."

All of those questioned played down their time at the camps. For example, Fanny Fritzsch, widow of Auschwitz prison camp leader Karl Fritzsch, had "no difficulties to explain the atrocities her husband was accused of. She had simply decided that they had never happened," Segev writes. According to Fanny Fritzsch, nobody died at Auschwitz. She told Segev that Fritzsch had been "the best husband on Earth," and that she had raised their children based on his model.

Ruth Irene Goeth stands out amongst the interviewees: True, she also plays down what Amon Goeth did, but at the same time she puts on a show as the profligate widow, downright wallowing in reminiscences of her time in the camp. Segev writes about his visit with Ruth Irene Goeth:

"In the late seventies, Ruth Goeth lived in an apartment that had seen better days. She received me in a Chinese wrap dress. Dark green velvet curtains covered in dust and heavy furniture gave the apartment a gloomy air. She sat down on the sofa, crossed her legs and—through a long holder—smoked one cigarette after another, her little finger coyly raised. It was a carefully staged performance; it was not difficult for the former actress to affect a nihilism that was evocative of Weimar Germany in the 1920s. 'Oh, well, Płaszów,' she said in a husky, raspy voice. 'Yes, yes, Płaszów.' She paused and then suddenly said: 'They will tell you that I had a horse there and that I was a whore. Indeed, I did keep company with a large number of officers, but only until I met Goeth. And he gave me a horse. I used to love riding then. Ah, Goeth—a picture of a man!' I could not help feeling that she enjoyed every single moment of her performance. . . .

"'It was a wonderful time', his widow said. 'We enjoyed each other's company. My Amon was king, I was his queen. Who wouldn't have relished that?' She added that she was only sorry it was all over."

As to Amon Goeth's victims, Ruth Irene Goeth adds: "They weren't really people like us. They were so filthy."

       ■   ■   ■

I AM STANDING AT THE TOP of the watchtower, looking out over the vast area of the Auschwitz-Birkenau concentration camp. "The size of at least 100 soccer fields," another tourist says next to me in German.

An icy wind is blowing around the tower. I think about zipping up my coat. The people here suffered terribly from the cold. Will I be better able to share their feelings, their desperation, if I keep my jacket open? Must I keep it open? Must I imagine what it was like being crammed double and triple into bunk beds, living in drafty barracks without heating or stoves, not being allowed to go to the toilet at night, and how they dealt with it if they were suffering from diarrhea?

Is there any point at all to my coming to Auschwitz—hasn't it all been written up in the history books anyway?

I've never been here before, but if I had to draw a picture of a concentration camp it would look like this. The gate to Auschwitz-Birkenau, the tracks that lead into the camp, the vast sky above the barracks. When I think of the words "concentration camp," I see the tracks of Birkenau in my head—and the faces of the emaciated people who were liberated from the camp, their large eyes set deeply in their sockets. These images are imprinted on most people's minds—and firmly fixed in my own.

I walk along the tracks until they end abruptly. Many of the people who climbed down from the cattle cars right here were already half-dead when they arrived. At the ramp, they were divided into two groups: one went straight to the gas chambers, and the other was forced to work. The trains from Płaszów probably arrived here, too.

The gas chambers and crematoria stood at the edge of the meadow, in front of the birches that Birkenau is named for. Shortly before their withdrawal in January 1945, the Nazis dismantled the buildings and demolished the last remaining crematorium.

Over a million people died here. We are walking over their ashes.

Some of my fellow travelers are asking lots of questions; I just listen. In the children's barracks, simple pictures have been drawn on the cold, bare walls. Pictures of a normal childhood: children with a doll, a toy drum, a wooden pull along pony. I am reminded of my own sons. These children here were alone, unprotected.

The tour guide hurries us along; we have to get back to the bus—we need to move on to Auschwitz I, the smaller main camp. A few minutes later we arrive, and I walk through the entrance gate displaying the motto "Arbeit Macht Frei"—"Work brings freedom." I recognize it immediately; I have seen it in photographs innumerable times. It feels strange walking through here now, unreal somehow.

When I visited the Płaszów memorial yesterday, I came not just as Jennifer Teege but also as the granddaughter of Amon Goeth.

My grandfather was the key figure there, so the place concerned me directly. Now, one day later in Auschwitz, I am but one visitor among many.

The tour of the fenced-in compound begins. The path takes us to the row of red brick buildings that house the museum's exhibits with their display cases, photos, and statistics. So many numbers. There is something impersonal about numbers; they confuse me. I prefer letters.

I walk from room to room, from one building to the next. I am not prepared for the room that I enter next: a huge pile of spectacles behind a glass wall. After that, a room full of shoes: boots, sandals, a lady's red slipper.

And then a mountain of human hair. Why must I suddenly recall my last haircut? Just a small amount of trimmed hair was left on the floor. Here, there are two tons. When the Red Army liberated the camp, they found seven tons of human hair, two of which are exhibited here. Seven tons of human hair, an inconceivable amount. The hair belonged to the murdered women and girls; it was destined for use in felt materials and sweaters.

More displays: crutches, prostheses, wooden legs, stilts, hairbrushes, shaving brushes. And pacifiers, baby clothes, two small wooden clogs, tiny knitted mittens.

Behind glass, suitcases with names and addresses written on them in chalk: Neubauer Gertrude, orphan. Albert Berger, Berlin. There is a Hamburg address, too.

I step into narrow walkways lined with row after row of photographs of the camp inmates. I enjoy photography, especially portraits. I like to get really close up so I don't miss anything. I study these photos closely. Some prisoners look proudly into the camera, others are frightened. Most of the faces wear vacant expressions. These are portraits of the dead.

In the beginning, the newly arrived prisoners were photographed; later, they were tattooed with identification numbers instead. The ink used to tattoo the prisoners was supplied by the Pelikan company. At school, we used to write with Pelikan fountain pens and Pelikan ink, and we never thought anything of it.

I go back outside, sit down on a bench, and take a few deep breaths of fresh air. I need a break and want to be on my own.

After a little while I rejoin my group. We visit the so-called "death block" next, hidden behind tall walls. Prisoners were shot in the yard. Nobody could see in from the outside, but the cries and the shots could be heard. I go down into the dark basement. There are narrow chambers within the walls: standing cells, too tight to sit down in. Prisoners had to crawl to get inside. After a day's work, four prisoners would have had to share one of these cells, standing up in the dark the whole night long. This was a punishment for so-called camp crimes. One prisoner, for example, was sentenced to seven nights in a standing cell for hiding a cap in his straw mattress for protection against the cold. The cells would not be opened again until the following morning. Sometimes a man would have died by then, and the other prisoners would have spent the night pressed tightly against his corpse. I push for more details. Who comes up with such cruelties? People like my grandfather. There were standing cells at Płaszów, too.

More and more visitors are pushing down into the cramped basement. People are pushing me from all sides, and I hasten back outside. In a way, it is a good thing that so many people come to Auschwitz, that they are not running away from history.

Near the office of former camp commandant Rudolf Hoess, we pass the gallows where Hoess was hanged after the war. The man who organized the mass murders at Auschwitz. I remember reading that, when Hoess and my grandfather were extradited to Poland together, the mob attacked Amon Goeth and wanted to lynch him. I was shocked. Their reaction illustrates the extent of the hatred people felt for my grandfather. It wasn't Spielberg's film that turned my grandfather into evil personified; he had already become a symbol of sadism while he was still alive.

A group of teenagers has gathered around the spot where Hoess was executed. I watch them from a distance and wonder what they are feeling right now. Anger? Gratification? Indifference?

One of the gas chambers avoided demolition, and one of the crematoria as well. The room is dark, the ceilings are low. I peer into the dark hole of the incinerator while, next to me, other tourists are filming the surreal surroundings with their cell phones.

And then it all becomes too much; I need to get away from Auschwitz. I feel as if I am being choked. This place is too dark, like a deep hole, like a grave that is pulling me in. I don't want to be sucked in. It doesn't help the victims or me if I only see myself as a perpetrator's granddaughter and only grieve and suffer as such. I'm glad I came here, but I'll never come back.

I wish someone had made my grandmother come and see this place. Surely, here, she would have had to open her eyes at last.

■　■　■

In the early 1980s, London filmmaker Jon Blair was working on a documentary about Oskar Schindler in agreement with Steven Spielberg. In doing so, Blair carried out much of the research that laid the foundation for the feature film *Schindler's List*. He talked with Schindler's widow Emilie and many survivors. Even 65-year-old Ruth Irene Goeth agreed to an interview, despite being very ill; she was suffering from pulmonary emphysema and was at times dependent on an oxygen tank. Ruth Irene Goeth expected Blair to come alone and to ask her about Oskar Schindler. Instead he rolled up with an entire film crew and asked questions about Amon Goeth. It was a long interview.

The video shows a well-groomed and made-up woman, her jet-black hair piled up high on her head, yet she is ravaged by her disease and constantly gasping for air. She speaks English and chooses her words carefully.

And she still defends Amon Goeth: "He was no brutal murderer. No more than the others. He was like everybody else in the SS. He killed a few Jews, yes, but not many. The camp was no fun park, of course."

She claims that, before the camp, Amon Goeth never had any dealings with Jews. She omits any mention of the bloody ghetto liquidations Amon Goeth organized before and during his time as commandant at Płaszów.

After the war, Ruth Irene Goeth was still in contact with Oskar Schindler, sporadically and on friendly terms. In the interview with Blair, she says that Schindler treated the Jews well, but mostly because they were useful to him. Schindler, Goeth, she herself—"we were all good Nazis," she says, "we couldn't be anything else." There had been no alternative, she claims; nobody liked the Jews—that was how they had been brought up.

When asked about herself, Ruth Irene Goeth explains: "I always felt that it was all wrong, but I wasn't the one who made the rules of those times. Whenever Amon and I had an argument, I would say that I was leaving; I didn't want to have to witness any more of this. But then the maids would come and say to me, please don't leave us, you always help us, what would we do without you?"

She describes herself as a guardian angel to those girls: "The whole camp was saying, 'God has sent us an angel.' And that angel was me."

When Blair observes that the only reason Ruth Irene Goeth had to protect the maids in the first place was because Amon Goeth would threaten and beat them, she counters that most people weren't treating their staff particularly well at the time.

In the end, it wasn't the maids' pleading that made her stay, it was her love for Amon Goeth. Ruth Irene says: "He was a very handsome man, well liked by everybody. He was obliging towards his friends, and he was charming—just not towards the prisoners, no, not at all." Amon Goeth had closer dealings with some inmates than others, and some he actually liked, she contends. But, she adds, there were so many Jews in the camp, it was impossible to know each and every one of them.

When pressed by Jon Blair, Ruth Irene Goeth admits that there were indeed old people and children in the camp, yet claims that she "never saw" the children. But then she recalls the children being deported, as already described to her daughter Monika—presumably when the trucks left Płaszów for Auschwitz. "Only once did I see that they were taking children away on a truck, and I was very sad; it tugged at my heartstrings. But a friend of mine said, 'They're only Jews.'"

When questioned by Blair whether she has any regrets about those times, she answers: "Yes, yes, honestly. But I never hurt anyone. Nobody can prove that I ever did anything wicked."

She claims that she never went inside the camp, never went near any of the barracks. She stayed in the villa, inside her "four small walls." From the villa, she was only able to see the prisoners in the quarry; they appeared to be completely normal workers, she argues. And no, she did not know that some of the workers died at the quarry. No, she never saw the executions that took place on the hill either, just a few hundred yards from her house.

Women forced to work at Płaszów

Shortly before her death, Ruth Irene Goeth showed her first signs of remorse. She told her daughter Monika: "I should have done more to help. Maybe my illness is God's punishment for not doing enough."

On January 29, 1983, the day after her interview with Jon Blair, Ruth Irene Goeth took an overdose of sleeping pills.

Perhaps Ruth Irene Goeth was afraid of what was to come once Jon Blair's documentary aired. Yet that certainly wasn't her main reason to commit suicide: She had first spoken of taking her own life months before the recording session.

In her suicide note to her daughter, Ruth Irene Goeth wrote: "Dear Monika . . . Please forgive me for all the mistakes I've made . . . I am leaving. I am a wreck. A burden to myself and everybody else. It is so hard to be locked up with this illness all by myself. I want to go to sleep and never wake up again. Everywhere I look, fear is staring back at me. Believe me, it wasn't an easy decision, but this life, being chained to the couch, is dreadful. Take care. Don't be so hard all the time. I have been so desperate. My life would have been one long illness. . . . Remember me well . . .

you didn't make it easy for me either. But I have always loved you as you love your own child. Your mother."

Not a single word about her time with Amon Goeth.

■　■　■

I CAN HARDLY WAIT TO SEE my grandmother in the documentary about Oskar Schindler; I haven't seen her for so long. Now I will be able to look at her on the screen. I borrow the film from the same library where I first found the book about my mother.

The film consists of a string of interviews that the director, Jon Blair, conducted with contemporary witnesses. I keep asking myself when my grandmother will make her appearance. I fast-forward and rewind but can't seem to find the segment. At last, at 17 minutes, my grandmother appears.

She sits on a chair, bolt upright, looking straight into the camera. Her face is beautiful with fine features. She still has something youthful about her. She looks just as I remember her. As if time had stood still.

What she says is of no importance—I am not listening, I'm just staring at her.

I have missed her.

Now she is struggling to breathe. I can hardly bear to watch her gasping for air. She is terminally ill. I feel sorry for her.

I rewind the film over and over and watch the scenes with my grandmother a second, third, and fourth time. Only later do I take in what she is saying. She is still defending herself. She has had time to reflect, but she is immovable. She hasn't changed.

I am sad and angry. Angry with her, but also with the people around her. They point the camera directly at my grandmother; she is obviously very ill, and yet they won't leave her in peace. Irene gives evasive answers; her English is excellent. Her voice sounds familiar, lovely. Like it used to. If only she wasn't saying these outrageous things. I hear her suppressed anger. She feels like she's been cornered.

Tomorrow she will be dead. Is she already thinking of the pills she is going to take? When did she start saving them up? Has she already got the typewriter ready for her suicide note? Or is it during the interview that she realizes the time has come, that she cannot escape her illness, or her past?

They bombard her with more and more questions. I can tell by the look on her face that she would like to be left alone, that she doesn't want to give any more answers. But the camera remains trained on her exhausted face. I watch her eyes; I like her eyes the best. They say that if you're lying, your eyes become evasive, flutter, look upward, away. But she doesn't look away. Her eyes look straight ahead. I don't catch her lying. That makes it even more painful: She really believes what she is saying.

Her suicide note doesn't mention the victims—it is all about her and her illness.

Also, her letter only mentions one child; she is referring to my mother's second daughter, my younger half-sister. I was adopted and therefore gone. Nevertheless, I believe that my grandmother was thinking about me right until the end.

I would like to have had a different grandfather. But I would choose her as my grandmother again.

Perhaps it would have been different if I had met her again when I was older. If I could have talked to her, if she had repeated the same family lies that made my mother's life so difficult. I'm sure my inner turmoil would be even worse. But I never discussed anything like that with her. I was just a child.

None of this means that I agree with what my grandmother did, or that I want to cover for her. I renounce what she did, and sadly didn't do, in the camp. I renounce her explanations. I simply distinguish between the public figure, Ruth Irene Goeth, and my grandmother, Irene.

Many children and grandchildren of Nazi criminals feel the need to apologize on behalf of their relatives. The grandchildren do this less fervently than the "penitent generation" of Nazi children. At first, I noticed the same response in myself, a fear of how my environment might react if I admitted that I love my grandmother.

The book about my mother is entitled *I Have to Love My Father, Don't I?* It implies that actually she mustn't love her father. The author, Matthias Kessler, keeps confronting my mother with her father's crimes. I can see him wagging his finger on the pages, can hear his judgmental undertone: You must not love this father, this monster!

But human psychology doesn't work like that. If my children were ever to commit some horrendous crime, I would condemn their actions resolutely—but I would never stop loving them.

The descendants of perpetrators are often accused of deluding themselves by constructing a psychological framework to help them deal with their ancestors' terrible crimes and to save the image of a good father or a good grandmother. Allegedly, they convince themselves that the offending relative was just acting on orders, that others committed atrocities of even greater magnitude. The descendants are said to cling to a fantasy that the culprit repented at the last minute.

I don't think this is true. I did wonder whether Amon Goeth might have eventually regretted his actions, but not in order to exonerate him—and therefore myself. It was much more because I am interested from a psychological point of view, and because I see

Amon Goeth as a human being after all. It is in our nature to have compassion.

My grandfather did not repent in the end; why else would he have raised his arm in a Hitler salute at the gallows? My grandmother never really repented either. She never really saw the victims; she walked through life with her eyes closed.

Nonetheless, I still feel close to my grandmother. I will not try to justify the fact; I won't explain it either. That's just the way it is.

When I was a little girl, she made me feel that I wasn't alone. I will always remember her for that.

Ruth Irene Goeth in 1983, shortly before her suicide

CHAPTER 4

LIVING WITH THE DEAD:

MY MOTHER MONIKA GOETH

This man, he dominated our entire lives.
Even though Amon Goeth was dead, he was still there.
—MONIKA GOETH IN 2002

WANT TO SEE MY MOTHER AGAIN, not for a reckoning, but for answers to all the questions I have going around in my head.

Almost twenty years have passed since we last met. Will she be surprised to hear from me now? Will she be shocked? Curious? Pleased?

Will she like me, or reject me?

I set myself a deadline; I wanted to contact my mother before the end of the year. It was October when I went to Krakow. November came and went. Now we're in December, and the weeks are quickly passing by.

By mid-December I can't run from it any longer. A week before Christmas, I write a letter to my mother. I have found her address in the phone book.

I stumble at the first hurdle. How should I address her? Mother? Monika? Dear Monika?

As a child I called her *Mama*, but that was a long time ago.

I start my letter with "Dear Monika" and wish her a merry Christmas. I tell her that I would love to see her in the new year. I give her my address and include a small photo of my husband and my two sons. I am sharing a small part of my life with her so she'll know a few things about me now: that I live in Hamburg and am married with two children.

I know so little about her, and yet so much—from the book about her, the documentary, and the Internet.

That was one of the reasons I went to Krakow—to be closer to my mother. She had gone there herself, tracing the steps of her own parents. It was there that she met with Helen Rosenzweig, Amon Goeth's former maid. In the documentary about that meeting my mother looks lost and lonely.

The journey to Poland was an important step for me; I felt much better afterward. The moment I laid flowers at the Płaszów memorial, I felt as if a huge weight was lifted from my shoulders. Since then, I have stopped busying myself with historical facts. When I close my eyes I no longer see my murdering grandfather before me, nor my grandmother gasping for air. I am able to devote myself back to my own life and my children.

By being able to take a step back, I may have achieved what my mother never managed to do.

I study my mother's photographs again. She looks so sad in some of them, her expression veiled, that it frightens me. I'm afraid these photos could pull me back into the depths of depression.

But without talking to my mother, I will never truly understand my family and my past. There are details only she can tell me.

At first, I wasn't sure I really wanted to see her again. After I found the book, all I wanted to do was shout at her and tell her how disappointed I was. How could she leave me, and then pretend that I didn't exist? How could she think it wasn't necessary to tell me the shocking details of our family history?

But I knew it would have been futile to contact her feeling like that. I would have confronted her in the role of a small, hurt child, unable to have a proper conversation.

I needed time to understand her better.

So I kept quiet. Only during my therapy sessions did I really allow my anger to boil up. My husband suggested I confront my mother sooner rather than later. He was angry with her, too, I could tell—maybe even more so than I.

Yet I considered it best to wait. I thought about my mother a lot. What kind of person is she? Difficult, an enigma. I pored over the photos I have of her, and I watched the documentary about her and Helen Rosenzweig with new eyes. She has a peculiar gait; her shoulders are hunched as if under a heavy burden. Now, I feel sorry for her. My anger has abated a little.

Looking at her life now, I can see why she didn't feel capable of bringing me up. I can even understand why she wouldn't talk about the past for so long.

Still I would like to hear it from her: Why did she give me away? And I want to know how she has been all these years.

I no longer see her simply as a mother who abandoned her child; now I see her as the daughter of Amon Goeth—the father who became the story of her life, the story that shaped her identity. That occupied her to such an extent that it left no room for other people, for her role as a mother, or for me.

■　　■　　■

Monika Goeth was born in Bad Toelz in Bavaria. Amon Goeth had arrived there in the confusion of the last days of the war, but he was soon arrested by the recently arrived American forces in May 1945. Ruth Irene Kalder followed him to Bavaria and gave birth to their daughter in November 1945.

While in prison, Amon Goeth wrote to Ruth Irene Kalder: "Dearest Ruth, at last we are allowed to write home. I have been thinking of you, especially in early November. Was it difficult, you poor thing? What is it—a boy or a girl? Hoping to see you . . ."

After the birth, Ruth Irene Kalder came down with scarlet fever, and Ruth's mother Agnes looked after her newborn granddaughter. For the first few weeks, due to the risk of infection, Ruth was only allowed to see her daughter behind glass. The distance between mother and daughter would always remain: Agnes became the person Monika would most closely relate to, she was the girl's "Oma." Her mother would always be simply "Ruth" or "Irene."

Much later, Monika Goeth talked about her childhood at length in an interview with Matthias Kessler, the author and documentary filmmaker.

When Monika was six months old, her mother was walking her in her baby carriage when a man suddenly attacked the carriage and stabbed the baby with a knife. Monika needed an operation; she was left with a scar on her neck. Ruth Irene Kalder assumed that it must have been a former inmate of Płaszów who tried to kill her daughter.

When Monika was ten months old, her father was hanged in Krakow.

That didn't stop Ruth Irene Kalder, who changed her name to Goeth in 1948, from romanticizing about her Amon, or "Mony" as he was called. Monika, also called "Moni," was in Frankfurt with her mother when she met with an old friend, Oskar Schindler. He took one look at the girl and exclaimed: "Just like her father!" Monika was pleased to hear it.

She wasn't suspicious until the day her mother shouted at her, during an argument, "You are just like your father, and one day you will end up like your father!" That was when Monika, now twelve years old, began asking questions. Her father had died in the war, hadn't he?

Her mother wouldn't explain anything. Eventually Monika managed to press her grandmother Agnes for the truth: "Well, they hanged him, you know. In Poland, where they had killed the Jews. Your father was one of them."

Jews? Monika didn't know any Jews. By then, the family had moved to Schwabing—the bohemian quarter of Munich—but even there in the big city Monika had heard nothing about the Holocaust. She would later describe the postwar atmosphere in the 1950s and '60s as a time when "people wouldn't talk about the Jews. They were extinct like the dinosaurs."

Monika pressed her grandmother for more information: "And where was Irene?" She replied: "Also in Poland."

The following day, Monika approached her schoolteacher and asked what had really happened with the Jews. The teacher told her to concentrate on her math homework instead of worrying about things that didn't concern her.

So Monika went back to her mother and probed for answers: How many Jews did her father kill, and why? Had he killed children, too?

When Monika wouldn't stop asking questions, her mother struck her.

Ruth Irene Goeth would downplay Goeth's actions and repeat the same story over and over: The camp Mony led was only a labor camp, not an extermination camp. Another commandant, Rudolf Hoess, had been in charge of a much bigger and much worse camp in Auschwitz. Ruth Irene Goeth assured her: There had been no children in Płaszów; she never saw a single child.

Ruth Irene also claimed that Amon Goeth had shot only a few Jews, and then only for "hygienic reasons." Monika Goeth quotes her mother as saying, "The Jews never went to the toilet, which caused diseases to spread. And when Amon once spotted a few men not using the toilet, he shot them."

Monika Goeth grew up surrounded by lies. She was a child, so she believed her mother. The words we hear as children take hold, and they keep flashing through our minds whether we want them to or not.

It would take Monika Goeth almost half a lifetime to find out the whole truth about her father and her family. She went on to read all the material she could find to help uncover the lies and half-truths in her head, a process that nearly drove her insane.

It took a lot of energy to tear down the web of lies her mother had created. It would have been easier not to, especially since the stories her mother had told her were feel-good stories—stories about a charming, loving, and witty father who ultimately hadn't done anything wrong. Looking back, Monika Goeth said, "I used to view my father as a victim—a victim of the Nazis, of Hitler, of Himmler."

Psychologist Peter Bruendl in Munich explains that, to ensure normal development, children need to grow up thinking, *My parents are good people:* "It is awful to have murderers for parents, to have to think, *me, a child of killers.* That's why many people accept their parents' silence on the subject, and they too keep quiet about it. They don't ask questions about what their parents actually did during the war."

The generation born in the years just before and after the end of the Third Reich came to realize that their parents would refuse to engage in any discussion of the Nazi years. Regardless of whether they had been SS men or common Wehrmacht soldiers, most fathers (and their wives or widows) would say little to nothing about the years before 1945. They left it to their children and grandchildren to eventually rediscover their family history. With the truth cloaked in silence, legends and prejudices flourished.

Agnes Kalder asked her granddaughter to let it rest, but Monika kept needling her mother. If Ruth Irene asked her daughter to clean the bathroom, Monika would reply, "I'm not your maid from Płaszów!" If her mother hit her, she would yell, "Don't stop! Come on, hit me again, you're just like the old man! It's not me who's like him, it's you!"

When Monika Goeth was in her twenties, she became friendly with a bartender at the Bungalow, her local bar. One day, when he rolled up his sleeves before doing the washing-up, he revealed a number tattooed on his forearm. Monika was aghast. "Manfred," she asked, "Are you Jewish? Were you sent to a concentration camp?" "Yes," he replied tersely. Monika wanted to know where he had been sent. Her questions made him uneasy, but he eventually admitted that he had been in Płaszów most of the time. Monika Goeth was relieved: "Goodness Manfred, am I glad that you were only in a labor camp and not in a proper concentration camp. You will know my father then; he was Amon Goeth."

When the bartender grasped what Monika had said, he turned pale. Much later, Monika Goeth would say that she could still hear his screams: "That murderer, that bastard!" Monika didn't understand: "But Manfred, you weren't in a concentration camp, it was only a labor camp, remember?" He didn't reply; he just stood there quivering. He wouldn't talk to her for days.

Monika Goeth urged her mother to meet her traumatized friend. Ruth Irene Goeth eventually agreed, but she wouldn't tell Monika much about their meeting. She only reported that Manfred had asked her again and again: "Why did you all do it?"

When she was barely 24 years old, Monika Goeth fell in love with a black student from Nigeria, a friend of one her mother's lodgers. Monika has described him as good looking, kind of a Harry Belafonte type. She moved in with him for a while, but the relationship was not to last. On June 29, 1970, Monika Goeth gave birth to a daughter; she called her Jennifer. Jennifer was given her mother's surname: Goeth.

At the time, Monika Goeth was working as a secretary, six days a week. She was also suffering from repeated episodes of mental illness.

When her daughter was four weeks old, Monika Goeth took Jennifer to Salberg House, a Catholic home for infants run by nuns just outside of Munich.

■ ■ ■

IT HAS BEEN THREE WEEKS since I sent the letter to my mother, and I still haven't heard back from her. I am worried that she might not get back to me at all. Maybe she doesn't want to get in touch.

In fact, that was another reason why I waited so long to contact her. I wanted to be strong enough to endure her silence.

The silence feels familiar. After my adoption she was suddenly out of the picture; I heard nothing from her, and I couldn't ask her anything anymore. Now, I try to stay calm. It took me so long to write my letter; maybe she needs time for hers.

Then, one Thursday, there is a call at my office. I am not there, so the caller leaves a message: Herr Such-and-Such would like to be called back. It was Dieter, my mother's second husband; he is about the same age as her. The last time I saw my mother, in my early twenties, she had him in tow. She had brought him along without asking me first. I would much rather have met with my mother alone.

And now it's Dieter who has gotten in touch, not my mother. I wonder why she didn't call herself. Is she sending him ahead?

The next day I call Dieter back. He tells me that he tried calling me at home but that I hadn't been in. We talk for a while until he asks me bluntly, "Why don't you simply pick up the phone and call your mother?"

Simply pick up the phone? For me, nothing is simple when it comes to my mother.

Still, my mind is already made up: I am going to call her. I need clarity at last, and I don't want to wait any longer. On Saturday my husband and the boys are out, so the house is quiet. I dial the area code, then her number. It's only a few digits, since she lives in a village.

I am nervous. It rings, once, twice, three times before she picks up. She says hello and tells me that she was very happy to receive my letter. It sounds as if she has been expecting my call.

Her voice is instantly familiar; it takes me right back to the days and weekends of my childhood when I visited her.

I like listening to her. I like the way she talks. She articulates very clearly and with long pauses. In public this can sometimes come across as theatrical.

Today I can hear the joy in her voice, but she also sounds nervous. I wonder where she is right now. I know that she lives in a single-family home. In the film about her meeting with Helen Rosenzweig, some of the scenes were filmed there.

Is she in the living room, in the hallway? Is she walking through the house with the phone in her hand? Or has she fled outside, to the fresh air? I cannot imagine her sitting on a chair somewhere; she is too impulsive for that. I am sure she'll want to be walking around. She's always been restless.

It used to make me nervous when I was a child. Her presence always brought tension to the air. I never knew what to expect from her next, which frightened me. She didn't speak much; in fact, the opposite was true—silence was her favorite form of punishment.

But today, on the phone, there's no stopping her. My mother is not at all surprised that I suddenly know about our family history. She assumes that I know about lots of things; she takes them for granted, jumping from one detail of her life to the next. In the end I ask her cautiously: "Can I come and see you? Would that be OK?" She replies without hesitation: "Of course!" When I ask her when would be a good time, she says, "For you, anytime."

When I put the receiver down, I am relieved. Given how long it took me to prepare for this talk with my mother, the call went well. She sounded happy and not hostile—that is more than I had expected.

We have agreed to meet up in February; I will go to see her in her hometown in Bavaria.

First, I travel to Munich. My adoptive parents have offered to take my sons skiing for three days, and I am staying at their house in Waldtrudering, to prepare myself for the meeting with my mother in peace and quiet.

Salberg House, the children's home where I spent the first three years of my life, is in Putzbrunn, a suburb of Munich, and only a few miles from Waldtrudering. I have driven past it on many occasions. Sometimes, I would stop outside, roll down the window, and contemplate the three-story, flat-roofed red building.

The house backs onto the woods. In front is a large yard with playground toys: a wooden ship for climbing on, a swinging bridge, a water pump. Today, a number of small children are outside playing and singing. Did we have these toys when I was here? I don't think so, everything looks brand new. As an adult I have only ever looked on from the outside, but today I'm going in.

■ ■ ■

Salberg House, a home for infants near Munich, was built in the 1960s. Until 1987, it was run by the Sisters of St. Francis, who lived in accommodations across the road. Compared to other homes, Salberg House had a good reputation. Government inspectors attested that the home was "well-managed." One inspection report further confirms that "the infants were evidently being well-fed and cared for. They all have a healthy complexion . . . The happy atmosphere in the home warrants a healthy development for the children."

These days, Salberg House predominantly looks after children who are in urgent need of a place to stay. Their parents are often incapable of looking after them; some have mental health problems, are addicted to drugs or alcohol, or are in trouble with the law. Some of the children have suffered physical or sexual abuse in their families. The children are brought here by CPS or the police.

In the seventies, it was normally the parents themselves who brought their children. Often it was single or working mothers who would ask Salberg House for help.

Back then, there was no such thing as parental leave in Germany: A few weeks after giving birth, mothers would have to report back to work; their jobs were rarely saved for longer. Many women would work full-time, six days a week. Part-time positions and childcare facilities were few and far between, and little assistance was available to mothers. Children were put up for adoption much more often than they are today.

Jennifer Goeth's case was no different. The reason for her admission to Salberg House in the summer of 1970 is listed in her files as "working mother."

In the early 1970s, up to 200 infants and toddlers were living in the home in Putzbrunn. They were divided into groups of ten to twelve children, each led by one or two nuns. The younger ones lived in the infant ward, the older ones in the toddler ward.

Today the groups have names such as "Bears," "Grasshoppers," and "Seven Dwarves." In the seventies, they were simply numbered. Today, the babies are walked about in baby carriages; back then, their cribs would have simply been pushed onto the balconies for fresh air. Wolfgang Pretzer, the current director at Salberg House, explains: "Even if it was a very good orphanage for its time, by today's standards it was more about the provision of daily essentials than actual care. In those days, they had less time to meet each child's individual needs. The groups were larger, and they had fewer care staff than we do today."

■ ■ ■

MY EARLIEST MEMORY IS OF LYING on the floor, screaming in the dark—I must have fallen out of my crib. The night nurse comes and picks me up and returns me to my bed. Tucked under my blanket, I go back to sleep.

We used to sleep in cribs with white bars; the sides could be lowered for access. One of the sisters must have forgotten to secure the bars after putting me to bed.

When I became pregnant and had babies of my own, I often thought back to the orphanage. For nine months, each of my sons was in my womb, safe and warm. Once they were newborns, I carried them around everywhere; I would sing to them and rock them to sleep. The close physical connection they had to me in the womb continued after they were born.

It was different for me; my mother just disappeared after my birth.

The photos I have from my time at the orphanage don't show it. I look happy in all of them.

The entrance hall of Salberg House looks friendly; the walls are plastered with colorful pictures drawn and painted by the children. I called in advance to explain that I used to live at the home more than three decades ago, that I would love to have a look around. The director and a female social worker who was there during the seventies have offered to guide me.

Despite the large number of children, it is quiet. We walk down long corridors and are met by a few toddlers coming toward us on tricycles and ride-on cars.

My group of children had been led by Sister Magdalena. My adoptive mother has told me about her, how lovely and approachable she was. The older woman remembers: "Sister Magdalena's group used to be in the room on the left by the stairs—where the Bears are now."

I am allowed to enter one of the groups' living rooms. First we have to ring the bell, just like at a normal home, before one of the care workers opens the door. There is a dining room with an open kitchen and a sunny, brightly furnished living room. Further along there are three bedrooms for two to three children each—the same size group as during my time here.

A little dark-haired girl with a pale face and rings under her eyes comes toward me. She shoots me a quick glance. I later learn from her caregiver that she hasn't said a word since she arrived. There are two dark-skinned girls, too, their frizzy curls sticking up; they are laughing.

I wonder what these children have been through. Do they miss their parents? Do they want to return to their families?

During my time at Salberg House, we had designated visiting hours on the weekends. Every Sunday, as the other children's moms and dads were arriving, I would look longingly at the door: Would my mother be coming today?

■　　■　　■

Monika Goeth would visit Jennifer only once in a while, and even then she did not always have time for the little girl. She had married a man who often beat her. Once, outside the orphanage, he beat her so hard that she

Jennifer Teege's christening in the orphanage's own chapel; the young Sister Magdalena is her godmother

needed hospital treatment. Jennifer got to know her mother's husband during her visits. Monika Goeth would later say about him: "My first husband was just like Amon. I must have chosen him to punish myself."

Sometimes, however, Monika would take Jennifer to Ruth Irene Goeth's apartment in Schwabing.

Jennifer was christened on March 21, 1971, in the chapel annexed to Salberg House. Her mother did not attend; Sister Magdalena was Jennifer's godmother.

■　■　■

I STEP INTO THE PLAIN LITTLE chapel where I was christened. I ask my guides for a moment on my own and sit down in a pew. In the living room of my adoptive family's home there is a table with a deep drawer. We children used to keep our photo albums in it. Among others, my photo album contains pictures of my christening, stuck in carefully by my adoptive mother. A young, blonde nun is holding me over the font—Sister Magdalena, my care worker and godmother. She is wearing the white habit of the order working at the orphanage. Next to her is the priest, pouring the baptismal water over my head. In another photo, Sister Magdalena is carrying me in her arms. I am wrapped in a long, white christening robe, my tiny dark hand gripping hers. In her floor-length habit and wimple Sister Magdalena looks like a Madonna.

I believe that she and her assistants did their utmost to ensure that, even though we were in an orphanage, we children would experience love and tenderness. She strove to be a kind of substitute mother for eleven young children. At bedtime she would pray with us in the dormitory.

I would love to meet with her, but she no longer lives in the convent. She once wrote a letter to my adoptive parents and said that she had left the order. She also mentioned that she had once caught sight of me and my new family in downtown Munich. She hadn't wanted to intrude at the time but hoped that I was still doing well.

With help from the Order of St. Francis, I manage to get ahold of Sister Magdalena's email address. I write to her and receive a prompt reply. She begins her email with "Dear Mrs. Teege—or dear Jenny?"

Sister Magdalena remembers me well. She still has many photographs of me, she writes. I should come and visit her; she and her husband don't live far from Munich.

I have no problems finding their detached home in the middle-class suburb. Sister Magdalena's hair is white now; she wears it in little curls. She welcomes me with a hug.

A plain cross hangs on the wall above the kitchen door; it catches my eye as I come in. God still plays an important role in her life, she explains, but the church much less so. After she left the order she got married and had children. Now she has grandchildren, too. Her husband joins us at the table. He used to be a priest, speaks several languages, and is originally from somewhere near Krakow. He knows Płaszów, and he has heard of Amon Goeth. As I tell them about my recent discoveries, they both listen intently.

Sister Magdalena has no memories of my mother or my grandmother. But she remembers that I used to be sad when nobody came to collect me on the weekends. Some children saw their parents frequently. She tells me that I had a friend in my group whose parents came to visit her every Sunday, and that I was keenly aware of it. In the early days my mother came regularly, she says, but as time went on her visits became more sporadic.

Magdalena was in her late twenties when she was my care worker. Now she is in her late sixties, but she still recalls many details. She says that I was a happy, open, uncomplicated child and very popular in my group. She had a personal relationship with each of her charges, and she is still in touch with some of them today. Very few of the children from the orphanage have had a straightforward life, she says; many are struggling.

She shows me her photo albums: Sister Magdalena and us at the zoo; Sister Magdalena and Santa at Salberg House. There was another dark-skinned girl in my group, as well as a number of children with physical disabilities; one was blind in one eye, another was missing a leg.

Magdalena says that her job was to give an "extra portion of love." She confides that she found it incredibly hard to let go of the children when their time had come to leave the home.

My reunion with Sister Magdalena is very happy and joyful. We talk and talk; I don't want to leave.

On my way back to my adoptive parents' house, I try to remember what it was like for me to suddenly find myself separated from Sister Magdalena. She was the person I felt closest to at the orphanage. One fateful day, I was taken in by a foster family, my future adoptive family, never to see Sister Magdalena again. Did I miss her? My adoptive parents tell me that in the early days I used to talk about her a lot.

■　　■　　■

The children of Salberg House usually left by the time they were three or four years old. By then, they were supposed to have been reunited with their natural families or placed in foster care. If they hadn't been, a different children's home would be found for them.

On the weekends, prospective parents would often come to Salberg House to choose a child to potentially foster or adopt. Cute little babies were the easiest to place. Jennifer was over three years old, and her skin was dark. "Back then, it was more difficult for black children. We wouldn't even have considered placing them somewhere in the country; it wouldn't have been fair to them," a former staff member recalls.

The first family Jennifer was introduced to already had a little girl and were considering a foster child of the same age. But when they saw Jennifer towering inches over the other three-year-olds, they decided against her: Jennifer was too tall for them.

At about the same time, a professional couple from Waltrudering, near

Munich, applied to foster a child: Inge and Gerhard Sieber. Inge is from Vienna and has a PhD in education; Gerhard, an economist, is from Bochum. They had had two sons in quick succession who were now three and four years old. They had been difficult births; both boys were born early.

Since they had always wanted three children, Gerhard Sieber suggested to his wife that they take in a foster child. This was nothing out of the ordinary for him; his sisters and his mother, who eventually became Oma Bochum to Jennifer, had given many foster children a temporary home. Gerhard Sieber considered helping children in need a lovely family tradition.

Inge Sieber speaks with a trace of a Viennese accent as she recalls her feelings at the time: "I was less sure than my husband. I was afraid that we might find ourselves with an emotionally damaged child and that I might not be able to cope."

In 1973, despite her concerns and with her two young sons in tow, Inge Sieber went to her local fostering authority and applied to foster a child. At the time, adoption was not on the table; all they wanted was to help a child for as long as it took. Inge Sieber explains: "To our minds, adoption was something for people who couldn't have children themselves. We already had two sons and didn't want to deprive a childless couple of the opportunity to adopt a child of their own.

"At the appointment, my two little boys were being so wild that I was convinced the agency would never allow us to foster a child. I was sure they were thinking, 'This mother can't even control her own children.'"

Yet the agency considered the Siebers suitable. A social worker visited the family in their home, and Inge Sieber had to undergo a health check. In those days, it was predominantly the future mothers who were checked, as it was assumed that the child would only be cared for by the woman. The Siebers' case was no different: Inge Sieber was a housewife and looked after her children; in her spare time, she volunteered in the neighborhood, supported the elderly in her community, and gave private tutoring in Latin.

Three months later, the Siebers received a phone call: "There is a mixed-race girl in a children's home in Putzbrunn who is in desperate need of a foster home."

Today it would be unthinkable, but the Siebers were put in touch with Salberg House without counseling or support of any kind. At the time, the fostering and adoption process was often railroaded through. Commenting on the practices of the early seventies, the chronicles of Salberg House state: "Prospective adoptive and foster parents would often show up at the door unannounced, proffering a letter from CPS that authorized them to inspect a certain child and to take the child home there and then. It took time and effort for the realization to take hold that it was in everybody's best interest for them to first spend some time getting to know each other."

Inge and Gerhard Sieber talked about the idea of fostering a child with their young sons. Matthias, the older of the two, remembers that his parents told them: "There is this little girl, and we're going to have a look at her."

When the Sieber family went to visit Jennifer for the first time, the boys had a picture book for her and a blue teddy bear. Inge Sieber recounts: "We saw a happy little girl with wild, spiky hair—the hair close to her head was growing in natural curls, but her mother had straightened the rest of her hair, so it stood up on end in spikes. Jenny was effectively presented to us—like some merchandise."

Another girl from the children's home immediately climbed onto Inge Sieber's lap, looked at her, and declared: "Mama, you are nice." Inge Sieber remembers how sad it made her that, to this little girl, a "mama" was any female visitor.

The Siebers took Jennifer for a walk and visited her a few more times after that. Eventually, Jennifer went for a "trial day" at the Siebers' home in Waldtrudering. For lunch, Inge Sieber served chicken. She says: "It appeared that Jenny was used to softer children's fare. She was surprised at the bones, picked at her food, and chewed the same mouthful over and over. I asked her, 'Don't you like it?' and Jenny replied: 'No, I don't eat cat!'"

For her afternoon nap, she slept in Matthias' bed; he temporarily moved to the guest bed to make space for her. Jennifer was a friendly and straightforward little girl, and she seemed to feel comfortable with the Siebers. At the end of the day, before they took Jennifer back to Salberg House, they asked the three-year-old, "Do you want to come live with us?" Jennifer said yes.

Inge Sieber went shopping with her sons to prepare for Jennifer's arrival. She bought a milk mug and asked Matthias and Manuel who it might be for. "For the little girl who is going to be our new sister soon," the boys replied.

On October 22, 1973, Inge Sieber collected Jennifer from Salberg House for the last time—to take her home. She was given Jennifer's health record with details of her vaccinations and which childhood diseases she'd had. Sister Magdalena gave her a collection of photographs. But one thing Jennifer did not have after three years in a children's home was a favorite stuffed animal or security blanket of her own.

Inge Sieber remembers: "The first thing I did was to take Jenny for a little walk. We went to the butcher's, and when he handed her a slice of pepperoni she beamed at him."

Frau Sieber was amazed at how "happy and mature" Jennifer was. She had been expecting a shy, traumatized, institutionalized child, but "Jenny was more confident and more independent than my own sons. She knew her way around everyday life. The social workers at Salberg House had prepared her well; they had taken the children grocery shopping in the village, for example."

One thing was unusual, however: At first, Jennifer would not leave Inge Sieber's side. She followed her foster mother wherever she went, even to the bathroom.

According to Inge Sieber, Jennifer was an inquisitive child, hungry for knowledge. When she saw Matthias and Manuel's toys, she asked: "Whose are those?" Inge Sieber replied: "They belong to all three of you."

Jennifer's older brother Matthias says that he and his brother were excited about their new playmate and that they liked her instantly. They never felt any jealousy toward their new sister, he adds.

Gerhard Sieber built triple bunk beds for the children. Jennifer slept in the bottom bunk; Manuel, who was about the same age as her, slept in the middle, and Matthias, who was one year older, slept on top. A photo from those early days shows all three of them laughing in their bunks: the two small, blond Sieber boys in red-and-blue striped pajamas, and thin, tall Jennifer in a nightdress made from the same material.

Every year on October 22, the anniversary of Jennifer's arrival in Waldtrudering, the family would give her a little present. "October twenty-second was something like Jennifer's name day for us," Inge Sieber explains.

■   ■   ■

I LOVE THAT PHOTO of the three of us in matching nightclothes, on the bunk beds.

After Inge and Gerhard had put us to bed, we would have our stuffed animals and dollies talk to each other for a while: Manuel's teddy—Grizzly—would growl, Matthias's teddy Rascal would interrupt, and Jimmy, my dark-skinned doll, would also chime in.

When we were tired, we would call out "Good–night–ev–ry–bo–dy!" We would take turns calling out the syllables one by one, and nobody was allowed to talk after that.

In another photo, we are standing proudly beneath the cross that stands at the summit of a mountain in the Austrian Alps, dressed in lederhosen and climbing boots.

My brothers and I became a unit very quickly. I felt very close to them immediately, and I still do today.

Having stayed at home with Inge for the first few weeks after my arrival in Waldtrudering, I soon wanted to join my new brothers at their preschool. I joined the same group as Manuel. In the mornings, the three of us trotted off together, collecting our friends on the way. Even though we were quite young, we usually went on our own. On the way home we always had to prove our courage: We would dare each other to walk closely along a fence, from behind which a big dog—we called him Buddy—would bark at us. My brothers would often send me ahead—I was the bravest of the three.

Waldtrudering is a quiet, middle-class suburb of Munich—a purely residential area where most of the dwellings are one-family homes surrounded by large gardens. The streets are named after German colonies and birds: Togo Street, Cameroon Street, Grouse Way, Birdsong Close. There are hardly any stores or businesses. It caused a stir when a McDonald's opened on the arterial highway that links Waldtrudering to downtown Munich.

For the first few years we lived in a first-floor apartment; then we moved to a single-family home. The rooms were small and full of nooks and crannies. The hallway and stairs were unheated; when you opened a door, ice-cold air would gush in.

In the new house, my brothers and I had a playroom for messy games, but mostly we would play outside in the fresh air. In the summer months, the garden would burst into flower, and a hammock would be strung between two trees. There was a soccer field not far from the house, and a hill. In the winter, we would meet up with other children from the neighborhood and go tobogganing down the hill, tumbling and shrieking with joy. In the evening we would collapse into our beds, hoarse and exhausted.

At the end of the road were fields and meadows, and beyond them lay the woods. We played hide-and-seek there, rode our bikes around, started a club, and built dens in the woods.

My adoptive parents took us children on mushroom-picking courses, where we were taught how to identify the various species of mushrooms found in the woods. For vacations we would go mountain-climbing in Austria or camping in Italy, usually with Inge's parents: our Oma Vienna and her husband.

I saw my mother less and less. In the beginning, she would bring me back to her place every so often, or take me to my grandmother Irene's. I only remember fragments of those meetings, but one occasion is still very fresh in my mind: My mother had collected me from my adoptive parents in Waldtrudering. We were in the car, driving toward Hasenbergl, the district in the north of Munich where my mother lived. We didn't talk much, and I spent most of the journey looking out the window. Then the first apartment buildings came into sight, rows of gray, uniform structures interspersed with public lawns.

When we reached the edge of the neighborhood, my mother parked her car. We got out and walked to her apartment. She darted ahead; I followed, dragging my weekend bag behind me. My mother opened the door, and we were greeted by her barking dog.

Before I had even entered the hall, my mother tossed the dog's leash to me and yelled: "Go take him for a walk!" Anxiously I set off. Outside, I hid from the children who were playing between the clotheslines. I hardly knew them, but they had teased me and called me "pickaninny" on previous occasions.

When I returned with her mutt, my mother dropped onto the sofa and lit a cigarette. She was still angry with me for taking the dog out only grudgingly. I sat down with her and asked: "Hey, Mama, what's up?" "Nothing's up," my mother replied.

■　■　■

Before they took Jennifer in, the Siebers had never spoken to Monika Goeth; they only knew about her from Jennifer's CPS file.

After Jennifer came to live with the Siebers, Monika Goeth would call them every now and then and arrange dates to collect Jennifer for a visit, or a visit with her grandmother. The Siebers, in turn, would inform Monika Goeth when anything had happened, such as when Jennifer had her tonsils out. They would give her notice before long family holidays, too.

Now, Jennifer had two "mamas," her foster mother, Inge Sieber, and her biological mother, Monika Goeth.

Inge and Gerhard Sieber had thought about what their foster daughter should call them. Their sons called them "Mama" and "Papa," and soon Jennifer did the same. Inge Sieber would refer to Monika Goeth as "the other mama," as in, "the other mama has got to go to work, that's why you're with us now."

Ruth Irene Goeth visited her granddaughter's foster family once, and the Siebers got on well with her. Monika Goeth, however, would come only to the front door when she picked Jennifer up. Inge Sieber never asked her inside. She found Monika Goeth to be reserved, and wasn't able to warm to her.

Today, Inge Sieber cannot understand why she never talked to Monika

Goeth about her daughter, especially because Jennifer was often restless and troubled after spending a weekend with her mother. "She never told us much about it," Inge Sieber says, "she only ever mentioned her grandmother or her mother's dog."

She recalls that once Monika Goeth did not even come in person to return her four-year-old daughter to her foster family; instead she sent the little girl back in a taxicab on her own.

When Jennifer was six years old, Monika Goeth was expecting a child with her then-husband Hagen. She consented to give Jennifer up for adoption—but not by any family, only by the Siebers.

Since Inge Sieber was not a German national—she is Austrian—the adoption process dragged on for nearly a year. Inge Sieber had to provide a number of references; friends and acquaintances testified that they thought she would do a good job.

For Jennifer and other children of her age, adoption was a complicated and abstract concept. One of Jennifer's little friends told her: "My mommy says that you're bedopted now, no, I mean redopted." And once, when Inge Sieber explained to Jennifer that it would have been physically impossible for her to give birth to Jennifer, because Manuel was only six months older, Jennifer reacted with a child's logic: "Then it's lucky that I was adopted, otherwise I wouldn't even have been born!"

Over the following three years, Monika Goeth kept sending letters and presents to her daughter, but Jennifer's adoptive parents only passed some of them on to her. When Monika Goeth heard nothing back from her daughter, she wrote a letter to the Siebers, asking if it was OK for her to get in touch every now and then, to keep sending letters and presents.

No, they replied—would she please refrain from contacting Jennifer? The girl was too torn between her natural and her adoptive family. It should wait until she was older.

They never heard from Monika Goeth again.

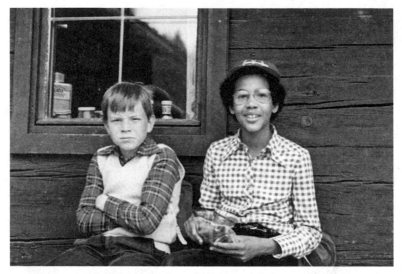

Jennifer Teege and her adoptive brother Matthias on a hiking trip in the mountains

Inge Sieber recalls that it didn't occur to her or her husband to stay in touch with Jennifer's biological mother after the adoption. "We thought that a clean break would be in Jenny's best interest. It was a no-brainer for us: on the day of the adoption, she became *our* daughter."

■   ■   ■

ON PAPER, I WAS A SIEBER NOW. In second grade I wrote a different name on my schoolbooks than I had in first grade. But my mother still belonged to me.

My adoptive parents thought it was best to act as if I really was their own child, as if I had always been theirs.

Yet our story together didn't begin until I was three. I came to them as a Goeth, and they were the Siebers. After the adoption, it was as if my mother had never existed. Suddenly, all contact with her stopped. She no longer called or came to pick me up for the weekend. What had happened? Had she forgotten about me?

My adoptive parents didn't say anything, or encourage me to talk about it. Quite the opposite: Inge and Gerhard seemed glad that I wasn't asking questions.

All they wanted was a normal family.

I didn't dare ask. Was I even allowed to? Wouldn't that mean that I was questioning my new parents? I wanted to belong to the Siebers. When they asked me, at age six, if I wanted to be adopted by them, I said yes.

All I wanted was a normal family, too.

Almost all the photos of my childhood show me laughing: buried in the sand on a beach in Italy, skiing with my brothers, eating ice cream, at the Oktoberfest.

Nevertheless, the smiling photographs don't tell the whole truth.

Early on, I knew: I was different. Different from Inge and Gerhard, my brothers, and the other children. A quick look in the mirror was enough.

Inge and Gerhard talked about me as "our daughter." I know they meant well, but often it was too much. At those words, others would stare at me, mouths agape, obviously asking themselves, "How can that be?" I pretended not to notice their surprised faces.

My childhood photos, the ones I like so much, all show two fair children and a dark one.

In the street, children sometimes called me names such as "Negerbub"—"black boy"—mistaking me for a boy due to my height and short, curly hair. I would quickly retort, "I am a mixed-race girl!" At birthday parties I always hoped nobody would look at me when they were handing out the Mallomars, which were called "Negro's Kisses" in Germany at the time.

At my preschool, I was the only child with dark skin, but in elementary school I met two girls who looked like me: sisters, their father black, their mother white. Just like me. I dreaded the thought that others might lump us together, so I kept my distance on the playground.

Later, in high school, there were two more dark-skinned, adopted children. Maybe I could have discussed my experience with them, but we only talked about everyday things. I had already internalized the silence.

My husband once suggested that we could take in a foster child. I don't know if I'd be able to cope with that. If we did, I would choose a child with darker skin, one who would look more like my own children, and be more likely to feel that they "fit in."

My adoptive parents were idealists. They did not worry about appearances; they just wanted to give a child a second chance. The first family I was introduced to rejected me because of my height; that would have been inconceivable for Inge and Gerhard.

I called Inge and Gerhard "Mama" and "Papa," just like my brothers did. At the time, those words rolled easily off my tongue. Once I became a mother myself, I started calling them "Oma Inge" and "Opa Gerhard." It felt more suitable. They loved being grandparents and were totally taken up by their new role.

After finding the book about my mother, I stopped calling them Mama and Papa. I felt it was important to distinguish between them and my biological parents.

As a young child, I could never say "adoptive parents" without feelings of shame; I never described myself as an "adoptive daughter." The word "adoptive" sounded like a flaw. I was uncertain of exactly what it meant, but I knew it was something awkward. I could look at the adoption certificate whenever I wanted—it was kept with other important documents in the desk—but we never talked about it in the family.

The adoption became a taboo subject.

I didn't even discuss my mother with my brothers, although we had a very close relationship: They were simply my brothers. With them, I could just be myself.

It was easier for them. Unlike my adoptive parents, they did not have to replace my natural parents, to compete with my mother.

Much is expected of foster and adoptive parents—to be and do everything that natural parents would, to become a strange child's mother and father as soon as the child arrives. Yet it takes time to grow into that role. In the beginning sympathy may prevail, as they feel sorry for the vulnerable little creature that has suddenly come to live under their roof. But getting to know the child's personality, and growing together as a family, takes time.

I did not take my adoptive parents' affection for granted. I was afraid I might lose it again.

Inge and Gerhard have always asserted that they love the three of us all the same. But I don't think that's possible. It *is* possible to love every child, but in different ways.

■ ■ ■

The younger of Jennifer Teege's adoptive brothers, Manuel, claims that he never saw Jennifer as his "adoptive sister." "She is my sister. Jenny has been with us for as long as I can remember." According to Matthias, her older brother, her adoption was in fact discussed, "but always in retrospect: That's how it was in the children's home, and then she came to live with us. The question of how Jenny might be feeling about it, or what her mother might be going through, was never addressed."

The subject was avoided, says Matthias, because it would have put a question mark over the siblings' equality. "That was our dogma: Everyone is treated equally. I only realized later that that wasn't the case." In reality, his parents had more trouble with Jennifer than with the boys. "They would argue a lot, partly because Jennifer was a girl. Our mother applied two different yardsticks; she was less tolerant with Jennifer. On the other hand, Jennifer could be undiplomatic. She would provoke our parents or rub them the wrong way."

Inge Sieber noticed it in her own mother: True, Oma Vienna fully accepted Jennifer, but she was always a little more reserved toward her than toward her biological grandchildren, Matthias and Manuel.

Inge Sieber attributes her difficulties with Jennifer to the fact that her new daughter came with a very different personality: "I am more of an anxious type—Jenny is vivacious and confident. I wanted her to come home on time, she insisted on her freedom. We fought so many battles."

■ ■ ■

ONCE, IN A CANDY STORE, when I was nine or ten years old, I slipped two little marzipan piglets into my pocket. I was caught red-handed by the sales clerk, who told me off in front of all the customers. She made me put the sweets back; my adoptive parents never found out.

A few months later, I pocketed a bag of chocolates in a supermarket. I got through the checkout without being stopped and ran toward the exit—straight into the arms of a large man, the store security guard. He steered me into a side room and made me empty my pockets, whereupon the chocolates came to the surface. He called my parents first, and then the police. I could already see myself sitting in a cell in handcuffs. After a while, Inge arrived.

Looking sad and embarrassed, she talked with the police officers and apologized to the guard. Inge and I drove home in silence. When Gerhard came home from the office, they summoned me to the living room and both gave me a severe dressing-down. I had to promise, hand over heart, that I would never shoplift again.

I went to bed worried sick that they would send me back to Salberg House. Like all abandoned children, I was traumatized by feelings of worthlessness. After all, my original parents hadn't found me loveable enough to keep.

My adoptive parents tried their hardest to be perfect parents, but they could not dispel my fear of being abandoned again. I thought that I had to earn their love over and over. I was missing a basic sense of trust.

One night, I dreamed that my brothers and I were sharing a peach: one half for each of them, which left me with just the stone.

It highlighted my underlying feeling: Whatever my brothers had was beyond my reach.

My adoptive parents set high store by performance and achievement. They taught us the importance of diligence and good grades from an early age. When Matthias was in fourth grade, he took an intelligence test. His results were outstanding; Inge and Gerhard were very proud.

Manuel was in my class. He was also one of the best students and achieved top grades in every subject. My own grades were so-so, and for many years I doubted my intelligence.

I must have been ten or eleven when one day I went hunting through the closets in my parents' bedroom. They weren't home, and I was hoping to discover some hidden Christmas presents.

What I found was a card with a gold chain and pendant. The card was signed, "Lots of love from Monika and little Charlotte."

Little Charlotte—that must be my younger half-sister, I thought, the girl my mother was about to have when she gave me up for adoption.

I did not confront my adoptive parents. I was too embarrassed for having rummaged through their closets.

At least now I knew that my mother was still thinking of me.

At age twelve or thirteen, during an argument with my parents, I demanded to be put in touch with my mother. Furiously, I declared that I wanted to see her again. My adoptive parents explained that I should wait until I was sixteen. Then I would be legally entitled to know my mother's address and to contact her if I so wished.

■　■　■

In the 1970s, it was common practice for adoptive parents to break all contact between their adopted child and the biological parents.

The realization that it is in the best interest of the child's development to deal openly with their past took hold only gradually. But every child has a right to know their origins; it even says so in the 1990 UN Convention on the Rights of the Child.

Today, adoptive parents are advised to explain the reasons for the adoption to their child from an early age, and to keep an album with photos of the child's natural parents, for example. It is also recommended that they find out as much as they can about the child's history. They have to be proactive, since many children don't dare to raise any questions themselves.

Nowadays, adoption clinics are more likely to discuss potential problems a child may encounter as a consequence of adoption. Studies have shown that adopted children are more likely than birth children to feel unloved, have self-doubt, crave recognition, and fear abandonment.

They are often afraid to commit and are more likely to suffer from severe depression and to seek psychiatric treatment.

Often, they will test their adoptive parents sorely: Will they still love me even if I behave really badly? Puberty, in particular, is liable to turn into an endurance test for the adoptive child and parents.

■　■　■

GERHARD AND INGE NEVER HEARD ME use the phrase that adopted children typically seem to shout at their parents: "You're not my real parents anyway, you can't tell me what to do!" It wouldn't even have occurred to me, since I was grateful to them. They had taken me in, given me a new life and a future.

But by the time I reached puberty, I was no longer content with just gratitude.

My rebellion against Inge and Gerhard was always partly driven by the question about my mother, by the question of who I really was.

At my adoptive family's dinner table, everybody had their place. Mine was on the left, in front of the windowsill with the flower-pots. But it wasn't only the seats that were set, our roles were as well: Manuel, blond and slim, was always best at everything, the highly intelligent one, while still being friendly and uncomplicated. He was closely followed by Matthias, equally strong at school, calm and bright, but less predictable than his ever-diplomatic brother.

My role was that of the fun-loving goose. When the dinner table conversation revolved around politics or culture, I turned away or yawned pointedly.

Chernobyl, the Cold War—those were the topics of the eighties.

Inge and Gerhard were very interested in politics. Inge was a member of Women for Peace, and the whole family joined anti-rearmament demonstrations. Gerhard, who had always been a loyal follower of the Social Democrats, voted for the Green Party for the first time. They went about saving energy and separating their trash for recycling with ardent zeal (I was the only one who refused to rinse my yogurt cups).

My brother Matthias was elected student body president at our high school. He was much more involved at school than I; he distributed flyers he'd printed himself and painted banners: a Pershing missile with an X through it.

Manuel was very interested in protecting the environment, too; he went on to study geoecology at college. His stickers proclaiming "Nuclear power? No thanks!" graced our bedroom door.

Eventually, we children each had our own bedroom. Mine had a pitched roof with a window opening onto the sky. I pushed my bed right under the window so that I could watch the clouds. I read a lot, spending hours up there with my books; I retreated into my own little world.

My room also served as a kind of "coffee house" where I would meet with my brothers. We would hang a sign on the door reading POD—short for "problem-oriented discussions," and talk about the things we weren't comfortable discussing with Inge and Gerhard: our friendships, broken hearts, fears, and dreams.

When I thought about my mother in those times, I would only recall her positive side; I'd suppress the bad. Lying in my bed at night, I would try to remember what she looked like and picture her long, dark hair. I envisioned her showing up at the door one day, taking me into her arms, stroking me. She would take me home, I fantasized, buy me expensive things, and allow me to do all the things my adoptive parents barred me from doing: wearing makeup or pantyhose, for example, or playing with Barbie dolls.

I soon wanted to get away from my family, from Germany. We weren't a normal family, yet no one seemed to notice but me. At 16 I went on my first vacation without my parents. On an InterRail pass, I crisscrossed Europe with a girlfriend, discovering Paris, Rome, and the Spanish island of Formentera by rail and by boat.

My late teenage years were more carefree than my childhood. I spent less time thinking about my mother and stopped brooding so much. Matthias' and my motto was *carpe diem*—seize the day. I had a large number of friends and went out most nights; I particularly enjoyed parties. On the weekends I worked at a club, the Skyscraper. A bouncer would check you out at the door; if you passed, you took an elevator to the top floor, which offered a sweeping view of Leopold Street, Schwabing's famous boulevard, below. Above the dance floor was a sliding roof; in the summer, people would dance under the open sky. I was 18; I worked behind the bar and thought that everyone there was ultra-cool, me included. I was not allowed to drink while at work, but I could smoke. I smoked like a chimney.

Then one day, when I was 20 and had recently graduated from high school, a girl named Charlotte called our home telephone. Matthias answered the call and took a message for me: "Some girl called Charlotte wants to talk to you." I remembered the card I had found in my parents' closet, and my mother's words: "Lots of love from Monika and little Charlotte."

My half-sister. The girl who had essentially "replaced" me: When my mother became pregnant with Charlotte, she gave me up for adoption. Charlotte came, I went. I did the math in my head: She had to be fourteen now.

I returned her call. A young, friendly voice. Charlotte explained that she would be visiting Munich soon, to see her father. Hagen—the man who beat my mother. He still haunts me in my dreams. Charlotte explained that he and my mother were now divorced.

Charlotte and I arranged to meet in a café the following evening. She had light brown, shoulder-length hair; she was wearing pants and a T-shirt. We talked for hours. She told me about her childhood and asked me, "Is your new family nice?"

She also described how she found out about me. By chance, she had discovered her mother's maternity log, with details of all her mother's pregnancies. Under "Children," she had spotted my name listed above hers. Charlotte ran to our mother and showed her the log. "Who is Jennifer?" she wanted to know. My mother claimed that I had died. Charlotte didn't believe her and probed further. In the end, my mother admitted that I wasn't dead. Only adopted.

My mother told Charlotte my new surname, which is how she found me and my brothers in the phonebook. (We children had our own landline because we would spend so much time on the phone.)

On impulse, Charlotte and I decided to meet again in two days' time. We drove to Starnberg and walked along the lakeshore. The sun was shining, and we spent the whole afternoon together. It was strange having a sister all of a sudden, but somehow it was nice, too. At the same time, I sensed that something wasn't quite right with her.

A few days after my meeting with Charlotte, my mother contacted my adoptive parents. She wanted to meet with me, preferably at our house in Waldtrudering. I didn't like that idea; it was too much—after all these years, I wanted to meet my mother on my own. I suggested that my mother could see just Inge and Gerhard first. I would wait to meet with her afterward, in a café downtown.

■ ■ ■

By the time Monika Goeth saw her daughter Jennifer in 1991, she had been divorced from her husband Hagen for several years. In the end, he had threatened her with a gun, and she had called the police.

She met her second husband, Dieter, at work: Monika worked as a secretary at one of Munich's universities. Dieter was very different from her first husband; he was calm, kind, and friendly. "Like winning the lottery," Monika said. After the wedding, Monika Goeth took on her husband's surname, by which she was known in private and in public from then on.

Dieter was soon offered a job in the country, and the family moved to a small village in Bavaria.

Charlotte started doing drugs at a young age. By her teen years, she was abusing heroin. She spent many years battling her addiction.

Monika Goeth brought Dieter along to the meeting with the Siebers. Inge and Gerhard had set up a table in their garden under the apple tree, and, together with Jennifer's eldest brother Matthias, they welcomed Monika and her husband into their home.

This time, Inge Sieber found Jennifer's mother more approachable. "She was very nice and said that she wished I could have adopted her too, that she would have had a better life then. I was pleased and touched by her praise." Matthias remembers the conversation as rather awkward and stilted. He recalls that Jennifer's mother seemed very nervous.

After a while, Inge Sieber told Monika Goeth: "You'd better go now, our daughter is waiting for you."

I HAD BEEN WAITING in the café on Wiener Platz in Munich for a while when a woman entered. A man was with her, and I nearly didn't recognize her: She had shoulder-length hair, dyed dark blonde. The last time I had seen her, 15 years ago, she'd had long, dark hair, which I liked better.

She was heading straight toward me. I got up. Uncertain of what to do, we shook hands. I was disappointed that she had brought her husband along. Why hadn't she come on her own? I had hoped for a private conversation.

Nevertheless, I was glad to see her again after all those years. I talked a lot, trying to make a good impression. I told her about my final exams, my recent trip to France, and my plans to visit a friend in Israel. She didn't comment on anything.

She remained guarded and hardly talked about herself. I didn't dare ask her any of the questions that were burning inside me: Why did you give me away? Why did I never see you or my grandmother again? What did Irene die of?

We had lost so much time, and now that we were sitting opposite each other, the distance seemed immense.

We parted with another formal handshake.

I hoped that we would see each other again soon, but my mother didn't call. Not after a week, not after a month, not after a year.

I didn't call her either. It wasn't a conscious decision; I just assumed that she would call me. After all, she was the mother. I didn't call Charlotte, either, since she was living with my mother.

Years after the meeting in the café, I was lying on the couch of the first therapist I saw for my depression. She asked about my mother, and suddenly my head started whirring. Like a film, my last meeting with my mother replayed before my eyes. And I got it at last: My mother didn't want anything to do with me, and she would never get in touch with me again.

Our "good-bye" in the café had not been open-ended. She hadn't forgotten to call me; she just didn't want to. Why not? Did I mean so little to her? For months, I went from grief to rage and back again, but worst of all was the sense of powerlessness.

When I first began to suffer from depression, there were days when I would sit for hours, the photo album from my earliest childhood on my knees, trying to remember everything. I went to Inge and Gerhard's and asked questions—questions I should have asked a long time ago. What was it like when my mother came to collect me? How did we greet each other? And when she dropped me off again, did I hug her before she left? Was there any affection at all? Did they know her violent husband? Inge and Gerhard seemed surprised that I would bring it up now, after all these years. They said that they could not recall any displays of affection between me and my mother, no hugging. They had never met her husband Hagen either.

For many years, I had to deal with those questions on my own. Every now and then I thought about contacting my mother, but I never did.

Now, I have finally written to her, we have spoken. On our phone call, I also asked her about my half-sister Charlotte. My mother gave me her phone number, so I called her and we arranged to meet. Again, I am going to see my sister before I meet with my mother.

I am stunned by how pretty Charlotte is. She is wearing her long hair loose, and she has a beautifully curved mouth. Her appearance belies the difficult years she has behind her. Again we talk about our different childhoods, about our mother. I have the impression that our conversation stirs up memories for Charlotte that she would rather keep blocked out. I witnessed my mother and Hagen's disastrous marriage on my childhood visits to Hasenbergl. Charlotte spent her entire childhood in that broken home; she experienced every row firsthand.

I realize that our conversation is taking a toll on her, and I feel sorry for her. I am enjoying seeing her again, but I am not sure if she feels the same. Am I asking too many questions? Or am I talking too much about my life, about my studies abroad, my travels— all the opportunities she never had? I don't want to hurt my sister.

I am getting angry with my mother again: Why didn't she protect Charlotte? But I have resolved not to be angry anymore. I want to meet my mother openly, without any reservations.

I would love to have a relationship with her. True, we have lived separate lives, but in the end we are still connected. I, too, have carried the burden of our family secret.

■ ■ ■

Jennifer Teege quickly understood that her grandfather was a criminal. It had taken her mother years to realize that.

Ruth Irene's suicide in 1983 changed Monika Goeth's view of her father, Amon Goeth: "Until then I had always fought against my father. After Irene's death I suddenly felt that I had to protect him—there was nobody else left who would have done that now. I wanted to accept Amon at last so that Irene could be at peace."

In 1994, *Schindler's List* came to German cinemas. Monika Goeth could not watch it to the end. Every time Amon Goeth—portrayed by the actor Ralph Fiennes—produced his pistol, Monika Goeth thought: "Stop it, just stop it!"

After watching the film, she stayed in bed for three days. Her husband called a doctor, who diagnosed a nervous breakdown.

Now Monika Goeth wanted to know all the details: She researched in archives, visited Krakow and Auschwitz again and again. She met with survivors from Płaszów. Monika did not walk to those meetings—she trudged there, burdened by guilt and shame and insecurity. Some survivors told her that they felt anxious near her, that they could not bear her presence since she looked so much like her father.

Regarding her father's deeds, Monika Goeth has said: "I believe all that, but I can't live with it. They hanged my father three times; my mother took her own life. I think that, surely, one day, my life will also come to a violent end."

Monika Goeth underwent a kind of public therapy—but not guided by a psychologist: The documentary filmmaker Matthias Kessler submitted her to a long, torturous interview, confronting her with her father's crimes. He would later turn it into a book with the title *I Have to Love My Father, Don't I?* It was that book that Jennifer Teege discovered in a library in Hamburg in the summer of 2008.

In 2006, filmmaker James Moll recorded the meeting between Monika Goeth and Płaszów survivor Helen Rosenzweig on film. Both women cried when they met in Płaszów. Their meeting is marked by misunderstandings, with Monika still repeating the phrases she grew up with: She explains to Helen Rosenzweig that Amon Goeth only shot Jews because they spread infectious diseases. Helen Rosenzweig is shocked. She interrupts Monika Goeth and asks: "Monika, please stop, stop right now." The film, *Inheritance*, first aired on German television in 2008, the day after Jennifer Teege found the book about her mother.

Monika Goeth later regretted her demeanor in James Moll's film. "I would never try to defend Amon again. I would just be quiet and listen to Helen."

Monika Goeth earned her high school diploma in her mid-forties; later she gained her Latin proficiency certificate and studied ancient Hebrew. She enjoys listening to Israeli music and has read almost all the standard works on the Holocaust. She is nearly 70 now, but she is still fighting the shadows of the past, every day.

■ ■ ■

IN A COUPLE OF HOURS I am going to meet with my mother.

I am feeling very apprehensive on my way there. I really hope that the curse that has overshadowed our family for so long can be lifted. That we will find peace at last.

My husband and I drive by flocks of sheep in green pastures as we near my mother's small town in the Bavarian countryside. He has come with me, but he won't be joining me for the meeting with my mother; he's going to wait in the hotel room. My mother is coming on her own, too. This time I want to see her alone, just mother and daughter.

We have arranged to meet in the restaurant of the small hotel where my husband and I are staying. I take a seat and wait. At the agreed time, there is no sign of her. At first I don't worry too much and use the extra time to gather my thoughts. But after a while I do begin to feel restless. I go outside to see if she is coming. A little later she arrives at last; she had been stuck in traffic. I am glad that she has made it at all.

This time she seems less like a stranger than when last we met, in the café in Munich when I was 20. I've seen her in the film, so I knew what to expect.

We talk about the little town where she lives, an easy, innocuous subject. Then she looks at me and declares that I remind her of my grandmother Irene—it's the way I dress, my handbag matching my shoes. It sounds like a reproach.

She mentions my grandmother, and, again and again, Amon Goeth—as if it were only recently that he was the commandant of Płaszów, only yesterday that my grandmother committed suicide. My mother says that she is living with the dead.

In an interview, she once admitted that having bad thoughts about Amon Goeth feels like she is betraying her mother, Irene, since he was the love of her mother's life. She believes that she has to be loyal to her mother, and that includes being loyal to Amon Goeth. That leaves her with a terrible dilemma.

Maybe that's the difference between the second and third generations, between my mother and me. My mind is freer than hers. I can have fond memories of my grandmother while also condemning Amon Goeth and my grandmother's life by his side.

I want to shake my mother and shout: "You are living now! Talk to me! Stop talking about your parents. Think about you and me! Don't look back, look ahead!"

I have read many books written by the descendants of Nazis. I understand that my mother's fate is not hers alone, but one that she shares with a whole generation of Nazi children. She is representative of this second generation. Many children of perpetrators have spent their whole lives suffering under their family history. Many have broken homes.

Seeing it like this makes it easier for me: My mother didn't give me away because there was something wrong with me, but because she had her hands full simply dealing with her own life.

The process of coming to terms with the Nazi era has always been a family affair.

The feelings the children of many infamous Nazis have toward their fathers range from glorification on one end of the scale to unbridled hatred on the other, and everything in between. Often, loathing for their fathers turns into self-loathing. The one thing they all have in common: They cannot escape the past.

Gudrun Burwitz, Heinrich Himmler's daughter, was an active neo-Nazi and collected donations for former Nazi criminals. Wolf-Ruediger Hess, son of Hitler's deputy Rudolf Hess, spent his whole life trying to clear his father's name. He proudly announced to his father in jail that his second grandchild had been born on "the Führer's birthday."

Bettina Goering, however, great-niece of Hermann Goering, Hitler's chief of the Luftwaffe, chose to be sterilized so that she would not "create another monster, not produce any more Goerings." Historian Tanja Hetzer says that, in interviews with Nazi descendants, she has learned of other men and women who chose sterilization or childlessness. "In this way, the Nazi ideology of 'worthy and worthless' life is propagated in the second and third generation and is, in an auto-aggressive way, directed toward their own offspring: They don't feel worthy to pass on their genes," Hetzer observes.

Niklas Frank, son of Hans Frank, Hitler's deputy in occupied Poland, carries a picture of a corpse in his wallet: It's a picture of his father with a broken neck, taken after he was hanged for his crimes. Frank says that, every night, he executes his parents afresh in his head, that they deserve it. In his book about his father, *In the Shadow of the Reich*, he writes: "I still feel like my father's puppet, he is still holding the strings in his hands."

Frank claims that his sister Brigitte "died from her father," as if he was an affliction. She committed suicide when she was 46 years old—the same age her father was when he was executed.

Many descendants of Nazi criminals are haunted their whole lives by images of their fathers.

There are many ways to distance oneself from such a father. Karl-Otto Saur Jr., for example, son of Albert Speer's confidant in the Reich's Ministry for Armaments and War Production, used to wear his hair long in defiance of his father's sharp, clean haircut. Monika Goeth studied ancient Hebrew.

■　　■　　■

TODAY, BETTINA GOERING LIVES IN NEW MEXICO. She speaks only in English and has kept her ex-husband's surname. I can understand not wanting to be called Goering, but her decision to be sterilized sends the wrong message. There is no Nazi gene.

I could not finish Niklas Frank's books about his parents, *In the Shadow of the Reich* and *My German Mother*. They may be important documents, but I didn't like them. They are not really about his parents; they are about his suffering from having those parents. Every line in the books is an infuriated cry, full of loathing and self-hatred. Yet all this hatred leads to nothing.

Holding on to the past does nothing to help the victims, nor does it aid in our analysis of—or coming to terms with—our Nazi past.

Ultimately, some children of perpetrators lose themselves behind their overpowering father figures. They define themselves by their past. But who are they when they step out of their fathers' and mothers' shadows? What is left of them? What do they stand for?

Malgorzata, the interpreter who accompanied me to my

grandfather's villa in Krakow, had also shown Niklas Frank and my mother around the house.

Niklas Frank resembles my mother, insofar as his parents became the central theme in his life. My mother is not as outspoken as he is, but I sense that she, too, believes that she has no right to her own life, no right to be happy. My mother believes that she has to atone for my grandfather's deeds, for my grandmother's looking the other way.

Constant self-flagellation and self-damnation will eventually make a person ill—and this kind of suffering, over one's identity and family history, gets passed on to one's children.

I have seen this firsthand in Israel, with Holocaust victims: They buried themselves in their pain and transferred their fears to the next generation. The trauma experienced by the child of a Holocaust survivor is totally different from that experienced by a child of a perpetrator, but the transfer process is similar.

I know that I don't want to live like my mother: arrested in the past, always in the shadow of Amon Goeth.

I think it's a good thing that people like Niklas Frank and my mother go into schools and give lectures about their parents, but that's not the path for me. One day I will tell my Israeli friends and their children my family history. I hope that I will be able to confide in them soon. I want to share my story with them.

I want to walk upright, to live a normal life. There is no such thing as inherited guilt. Everybody has the right to their own life story.

■   ■   ■

The third generation of Nazi descendants usually looks back upon their family with more detachment and fewer false justifications.

The children are still struggling to grasp their fathers' crimes—the grandchildren are trying to come to terms with their family's involvement. They analyze the oft-repeated family legends, investigate what is true and what was contorted or concealed.

The grandfathers' deeds—and especially the silence surrounding those deeds—impacts families to this day. According to the historian Wolfgang Benz, a report on "the history of the mentality of National Socialism and its enduring consequences" is yet to be written.

Historians talk of a "family conspiracy of silence." Katrin Himmler, great-niece of SS chief Heinrich Himmler, refers to the half-truths handed down in her family as "thought prisons." She was able to use her own research to show that Himmler's family directly profited from his position and that some members actively supported his genocidal policies, including her own grandfather, Heinrich Himmler's brother.

Other grandchildren advocate the idea of treating the past as the past. Writer Ferdinand von Schirach, son of Reich Youth Leader Baldur von Schirach, drew a definite line under his grandfather's history in his article for the German news magazine *Der Spiegel*:

"My grandfather's guilt is my grandfather's guilt. Our Federal Supreme Court defines guilt as the result of one person's individual actions. . . . I am more interested in our world today. I write about postwar justice, about German courts who passed cruel judgments, about the judges who sentenced Nazi criminals to five minutes in jail for each murder they committed. . . . We think that we are safe, but the opposite is the case: We can lose our freedom, and then we'd lose everything. It is our life now, our responsibility. . . . 'You are who you are,' that's the only answer I can give people who ask about my grandfather. It took me a long time to find it."

I DON'T THINK WE DESCENDANTS CAN disengage entirely from our past; it impacts us whether we like it or not.

I have studied the biographies of many Nazi descendants. The third generation no longer denies what happened under the Third Reich; they speak frankly about it. Nonetheless, some of those stories are lacking something: The people disappear behind the facts, they remain strangers. For me, they are too theoretical in examining their families' past; I find it difficult to identify with them. Dealing with the sins of one's parents and grandparents can destroy families; it is not an academic exercise.

And it doesn't stop here: The past will have an impact on my children, too. My two sons are still young. In a few years, they may well watch *Schindler's List* at school. I don't want them to be ashamed; instead, I hope that they will talk openly about their family history.

I think that we can only get square with our past and truly leave it behind us if we deal with it openly. Feeling that you have to hide yourself and your identity will only make you ill.

That is why I was so shocked when I discovered what my mother had concealed from me: The secrecy that overshadowed her childhood, her youth, her entire life—she let me grow up with it, too. I found out about it much too late.

I'm desperate for her to appreciate my despair, to understand the sadness that I have lived with all these years—to see what a relief it would have been for me to know the history of my natural family.

My mother and I have been talking for over two hours now—and not a word about us. Cautiously, I try to steer her away from the subject of the Holocaust and ask about my childhood.

My mother tells me that she moved back in with my grandmother Irene when she became pregnant with me. The two women discussed the option of my staying with them in their apartment. The children's home was only meant as a temporary measure, my mother explains.

After I was born, she adds, she struggled to bond with me. My grandmother, on the other hand, was immediately taken with me, and she often pointed out what an extremely good grandchild I was, that I never cried or whined. My grandmother loved taking me out on walks or grocery shopping, my mother recalls. Irene, a striking figure herself, enjoyed showing off her black grandchild, like a baby doll. She loved my exotic appearance. Even Lulu, my grandmother's transvestite lodger, would proudly push me around the English Garden in my stroller.

For the first time, I learn the inspiration for my given names: My name is Jennifer Annette Susanne. My mother explains that "Jennifer" was a vestige from the American occupying forces after the war. She liked that it sounded foreign.

"Annette" was my grandmother's suggestion; she just really liked the name.

"Susanne" was in honor of "Susanna" from Płaszów—since Amon Goeth had two maids named Helen, he called Helen Hirsch "Lena" and Helen Rosenzweig "Susanna."

After the war, my grandmother would often talk about her maids in Płaszów. When she was a child, my mother believed that Lena and Susanna were relations of some sort. Only years later did she discover that the years they spent in my grandfather's villa must have been the worst time of their lives.

So, I was named "Susanne" after a Jewish concentration camp

survivor—after the woman who meets with my mother in Krakow in the documentary that I watched so avidly, after the woman whose story moved me so much.

I ask my mother about my adoption. She tells me that it first occurred to her to have the Siebers adopt me when I told her that I wanted to have the same surname as my brothers. She adds that she discussed the matter with my grandmother Irene and that she said, "Sure, why not? I've met the family and they seemed very nice."

For my mother, the adoption was a mere formality. She thought that it would cut the red tape and make things easier for me and my adoptive parents. It was not until afterward that she realized it also meant she had relinquished her visiting rights. She tells me that she was angry and disappointed when she found out.

Once she was not allowed to see me anymore, she would sometimes drive past our house in Waldtrudering, and on occasion my grandmother would come with her.

My mother would look at the big, beautiful home where I now lived and tell herself that it was probably for the best, that she really couldn't ask for more.

She came to terms with the adoption.

My mother only noticed the outward appearances: the house, the garden, the trappings of a middle-class lifestyle. She didn't see how torn I was feeling inside.

She still doesn't see it. She doesn't ask me what life was like with my new family, if there was anything I missed, or if I missed her.

For her, it seems obvious: The adoption was in my best interest. I had a picture-perfect childhood.

She thinks that it was good for me to no longer bear the name

"Goeth," nor the burden of the family history that came with it. She still doesn't see that not knowing was the greater burden.

We talk for nearly four hours. She is learning ancient Hebrew, but she doesn't ask me what it was like living in Israel.

I am trying to put myself in her shoes, to be as careful and understanding as I can, to not ask too much. I turn into the mother, she becomes the child: I feel the need to protect her and help her.

My mother has invited my husband and me to dinner that evening. Her house is in a small hamlet near some woodlands. The garden is immaculately kept; my mother evidently enjoys her gardening.

When my husband and I arrive, my mother and Dieter are still in the kitchen preparing dinner. We share a bottle of wine in the kitchen before sitting down at the dinner table to talk. It is the first time that my husband has met my mother. He, too, notices that her conversation revolves mainly around her parents.

My mother tells us that she once asked Irene: "Why couldn't Oskar Schindler have been my father? Why did it have to be Amon?" And Irene replied: "You wouldn't exist if Oskar had been your father."

Once again, my mother compares me to Irene, but this time it sounds more favorable.

As we are looking together at photographs of my grandmother, she suddenly says: "Pick one for yourself!" I select one that shows Irene in profile; she looks just as I remember her, elegant yet natural, with a scarf draped around her shoulders.

My mother hands me the picture, and then she gives me a small cigar box. I open it up and find my grandmother's favorite golden bangle inside. My mother says: "It's yours." I love the unassuming piece instantly, but I hesitate: I don't want anything from the camp, nothing stolen, no gold from the teeth of the victims. On hearing that the bangle originally belonged to my great-grand-mother, I accept it gladly. The gesture makes me happy.

I am accepting of the fact that my mother talks almost exclusively about the past. I think, at the time, that this meeting is just the beginning.

When we arrived, she greeted me with a handshake. As we are leaving, she gives me a brief hug.

I have a mother now.

■   ■   ■

A few days later, Jennifer Teege is smiling as she talks about her reunion with her mother. She is wearing her grandmother's bangle on her arm.

Jennifer's older brother Matthias says: "After the meeting with her mother, Jenny's natural family was at the forefront of her thinking. She questioned the time she'd spent with her adoptive family."

Inge Sieber experiences this as "Jennifer detaching herself from her family a second time, after puberty: After her reunion with her mother she was very critical of us; that was very hard for my husband and me." It was hard enough for Inge Sieber when, after she discovered the book, Jennifer started calling her by her first name instead of "Mama": "That hurt me deeply." Only sometimes, she adds, does Jennifer forget and call her "Mama" again.

A second meeting with her mother is arranged, this time including her sister Charlotte, too. Once again, Jennifer and her family are staying with her adoptive parents in Waldtrudering.

Her adoptive father, Gerhard, takes Jennifer's sons for a walk in the garden. He has recently planted two trees there especially for them—a gingko for Claudius and an apple tree for Linus. Now he is showing them to his grandsons. "Opa, we're going to meet Mama's mama today," Jennifer's younger son Linus announces.

As Jennifer Teege, her husband, and her sons set off, Jennifer's adoptive parents wave good-bye.

■ ■ ■

I AM LOOKING FORWARD TO SEEING my mother again. This time, Charlotte will be coming, too, and my husband and our children. A Good Friday out with my family. My family: It sounds authentic when I say it like that.

I wish there was more lightness in these relationships. I hope that we can get beyond the point where all we talk about is our family legacy. It would be nice to just go out together and have fun.

I once said half-jokingly to Charlotte: "Maybe one day we'll spend Christmas together!" I don't think that that will ever happen. I have my adoptive family; they will always be there. But it would be lovely if my mother and Charlotte could become part of my life, too.

My mother has a great opportunity now: After all these years, she can have her daughter back.

It was interesting to talk with my mother on her own; I learned so much about her and my grandmother. I could even fit some of the long-missing pieces into the jigsaw puzzle of my life.

I already knew some of the things she told me from the book about her, but now there is a new character in her story: me. It had hurt me deeply that there was no mention of me in the book. She says that was to protect me, to enable me to have a new life.

She is not the type to question her own actions; she lives too much in her own world for that. She often comes across as aloof and says things that sound harsh and absolute. But I believe that, behind the façade, there lies a woman in need of love, and worthy of love.

I can see the path she has taken: Emotionally, she hit rock bottom over and over again. She had a terrible first marriage—and now she is leading a nearly normal life. I think she keeps many things at a distance deliberately, to protect herself.

My husband parks the car in front of the restaurant where we have arranged to meet. We get out of the car. Charlotte arrives; she looks exhausted. She notices the golden bangle on my arm, and I tell her that our mother gave it to me, that it is from Irene. Charlotte stares at the bangle but says nothing.

My mother and Dieter arrive, and we have lunch together. Afterward, we go for a walk in the English Garden. We hire rowing boats on the lake in the park and later take the children to the playground.

Outwardly it looks like an ordinary get-together, but the atmosphere is quite strained. I would have liked it to be more lighthearted, more personal. I had hoped to get to know Monika as my mother, not just as an older woman. After our first meeting, I still thought that might be possible. Now I am being more realistic; I sense that my mother does not crave a close relationship as much as I do. It's partly due to her personality—she doesn't have a strong maternal side.

I am 40 years old now, she is 64. I am too old for mother-daughter bonding. She cannot give me my bottle or hold my hand while I take my first steps. All those things that she's missed—that we've both missed—we can't make up for them now.

I see my mother one more time, four days after our day out on Good Friday. We meet at my grandmother's grave.

I had asked her to take me to Irene's burial place; I felt a real need to go there with her. We agree to meet at the Viktualien-markt, a popular market for flowers and delicacies in the center of Munich. I buy some flowers and we head to the Nordfriedhof, Schwabing's cemetery. My mother visits the grave regularly; it seems that she has made peace with her mother now.

We walk through the entrance gate. The cemetery is vast. There are tall, ancient trees, and narrow paths winding their way between the graves. Irene is buried in the same plot as her mother, Agnes Kalder. It is a beautiful grave, very simple. My mother and I plant a few pansies together. This visit means so much to me. In front of Irene's grave, I appeal to my mother: "If you should decide one day that you don't want to see me anymore, I will respect your decision. But please say good-bye and don't just disappear like you did when I was little."

We talk on the phone a few more times after that, and then I don't hear from her anymore. I send her a little package, but it comes back three times with a note: "Refused delivery." When I call her number, no one answers. I let it ring and ring—in vain.

■　■　■

The sign on Monika Goeth's front door says SHALOM. It means "peace," but there is no peace here.

Months after her visit to the Nordfriedhof with Jennifer, Monika Goeth is sitting on her patio, under a roof of wild vines. Her husband has baked a cake and made coffee. It is a warm, late summer's day; even the flies have come out again. Monika Goeth is talking nonstop, and every now and then she swats one of the little bugs. Digressing wildly, she tells her story, which revolves around one thing only: her parents, "Amon and

Ruth." Sometimes she is calm and smiling, and other times she furiously rants and raves about her screwed-up family.

Monika Goeth says that she has always tried to protect her daughter Jennifer, to keep her out of that whole "Goeth rubbish."

Monika sees Jennifer, first and foremost, as the daughter of her adoptive parents. Jennifer already has a brilliant mother, she asserts—what does she want from me all of a sudden?

Monika Goeth says that, in her eyes, the people who bring a child up are the parents.

She doesn't understand what this strange daughter wants from her, why she clings to the notion that even a terrible truth is better than silence, that a broken family is better than no roots at all.

Monika Goeth says that she was very pleased to hear from Jennifer initially, but adds that her daughter moves at a different pace. She explains how she felt downright harassed by Jennifer's eager desire to fix everything, to reunite the family. She felt as if Jennifer had written a script for a reconciliation scene that they were supposed to act out with all speed. But it takes time to develop a relationship after so many years, and in the end, she adds, she felt that it was too late.

Jennifer Teege will only ever see her mother again on TV. Monika Goeth has been giving fresh interviews; an Israeli documentary-maker has persuaded her to talk about her role as Amon Goeth's daughter. Time and again, Monika Goeth finds herself in the public eye, even though all she wants, she says, is to be left in peace.

Monika Goeth is now raising her grandchild, her daughter Charlotte's son, who is living with her. Monika says: "He is my life. I do the things for him that I would have loved to do for my father when he was a little boy."

Charlotte chose a traditional Jewish name for her son and combined it with her grandfather's, "Amon"—that is the middle name Jennifer Teege's half-sister gave her son.

I HAVE ALWAYS FELT that I am part of a mobile: everyone connected to everyone else by many invisible strings. If one moves, the others move as well. I am right at the bottom; the main characters are moving around above me.

The central figure is Amon Goeth; he is the source of this evil. Despite being long dead, he makes his presence felt, pulling the strings in the background. My adoption allowed me to escape the family system for a while. I had some peaceful years, but nevertheless I am, and always will be, a part of the whole, an important figure at the end of one string.

I wanted to disentangle the old ties and free our movements today, so we'll be able to adjust to whatever crisis comes next—and all pull through it together.

Maybe I was being too ambitious.

My grandmother's portrait, in its silver frame, takes pride of place on a windowsill in our house, next to photographs of my children and my friends.

Sometimes I visit Irene's grave. I take fresh flowers and light a memorial candle. I don't want to change much here: What would my mother say? After all, she has been caring for the grave for years.

The last time I went, the headstone was overgrown with brambles, but I didn't dare cut them back.

CHAPTER 5

GRANDCHILDREN OF THE VICTIMS:

MY FRIENDS IN ISRAEL

Where are you from—Obama family, eh?

—A JERUSALEM SPICE TRADER TALKING TO
JENNIFER TEEGE IN 2011

AM BACK IN ISRAEL. AT LAST.

Tel Aviv has grown: The highways seem twice as wide; new high-rise buildings loom against the sky. Many buildings in the city center remain dilapidated, their façades dirty, corroded from pollution and the salty air. Next to them, the recently renovated buildings gleam all the more brightly.

On Rehov Engel, a small, quiet side street, the house where I shared an apartment in my early twenties lies nestled between palm trees and flowering shrubs. This is where I sat in front of the TV all those years ago and watched *Schindler's List*.

The sun, the salty air, the throaty Hebrew sounds—it's all very familiar. But I am a different person now.

When I arrived here over twenty years ago to visit my friend Noa, I was young, curious, and unburdened. Now I am returning as the granddaughter of Amon Goeth.

Noa was the reason I came to Israel in the first place. She is also the reason I haven't dared to come back here in the three years since I discovered my family's past.

I first met Noa in Paris. After my graduation from high school in 1990, I moved to the French capital for a year. I minded the children of a French family, and I attended classes at the Sorbonne and at an art college, where I was developing a portfolio. I planned to study graphic or communication design on my return from Paris.

I met Noa in a life drawing class. We were both trying very hard to get the model's proportions right. After class ended, we stood in the corridor and talked for a long time.

I liked her quick wit and her sense of humor. She had long, curly blonde hair and light green eyes. She talked openly about herself and her feelings. Noa told me she sometimes had days that were somehow different—she called them her "camera days." I knew what she meant; I also have days where I feel like I am walking through life as a silent observer, zooming in and out on the world. Noa was able to give a name to the feeling that I had always found so hard to put into words. I liked her precise language and her unique view of the world.

Noa was in her early twenties, like me, and she was in Paris to accompany her father, an artist who had been granted a scholarship there. Noa's father always wore black clothes in winter and white only in the summer.

Noa's mother was a lawyer. She had worked in Germany, even in Munich. As a teenager, Noa had tagged along with her mother a number of times. Now she was trying to remember the few German words she had picked up at the time: "Bitte. Danke. Guten Tag."

She wrote down the Hebrew alphabet on a paper napkin for me. I was surprised to learn that words were written from right to left. Noa talked about Israel as if it were a perfectly normal country.

After my year in Paris, I returned home. I hadn't been accepted at any of the various colleges where I had applied to study design. I decided to visit Noa in Tel Aviv. When we had said our good-byes in Paris, she had asked me: "When are you coming to Israel?"

It was a four-hour flight from Munich to Tel Aviv. Noa was waiting for me in her apartment. She beamed at me when she opened the door and briefly showed me her room, which I was going to share with her. Her roommate, Anat, was sitting on the balcony. She was a little older than Noa, with strawberry blonde hair. "Anat, this is Jenny," said Noa by way of introduction. Anat and I shook hands. Soon Noa was eager to go out: She wanted to celebrate our reunion somewhere special.

Noa hailed a taxicab, and we drove along the promenade toward the south of Tel Aviv. After half an hour, the cab stopped along a gravel path. I got out and looked around: We were standing on a cliff top, the sea below us. In front of us was an open-air bar, full to bursting.

The bar, Turquoise, had deck chairs and swing seats on the lawn. More and more people were streaming inside. I thought the women were stunningly beautiful; almost all of them had long, dark, curly hair.

In hindsight, it is difficult to say what I had been expecting, but it certainly wasn't this: carefree people enjoying themselves, sitting in swing seats surrounded by palm trees and brightly colored beach umbrellas, listening to chill-out music, and looking out to sea.

Primed by my history lessons and news reporting about Israel, I had been prepared for a permanent state of emergency. I was thinking Holocaust and intifada (the Palestinian rebellion against the Israeli occupation). I had expected a traumatized people—in a country where bombs could explode anywhere and anytime.

I found a city built on sand, its bright apartment blocks on stilts in order to allow the fresh sea breeze to fan the city streets. I had expected heaviness and found lightness instead. That afternoon I knew: *I want to stay here, in this country.* Noa and I sat down on the warm grass. We watched the sun as it set slowly over the sea.

■ ■ ■

Tel Aviv means "Hill of Spring." It got its name in 1909, when Jewish immigrants founded a small settlement in the sand dunes by the Mediterranean Sea.

In the years following 1933, many European Jews sought refuge in Palestine. They wanted a country of their own, because in so many other countries they feared for their lives.

The first wave was of refugees who were able to flee Germany and the territories occupied by German troops in time.

Others did not escape from the Nazis. They came to Palestine after the war, mentally and physically broken by their experiences in camps like Płaszów.

The exhibition rooms at Yad Vashem, Jerusalem's Holocaust memorial, are deliberately kept in semidarkness. Visitors are presented with evidence and testimonials of Nazi crimes, among them a photograph of concentration camp commandant Amon Goeth, sitting astride his white horse in his SS uniform. There are more pictures of other commandants and other concentration camps—at last, visitors grasp the extent of the killings. And then the corridor leads them slightly uphill to the exit, where they emerge into a sun-drenched Israel. This is Yad Vashem's message: Israel and the Holocaust are like day and night. The new country is the emergence into light.

On May 14, 1948, Zionist leader David Ben-Gurion proclaimed the establishment of the state of Israel in Tel Aviv. That day, the Jews danced with joy on Dizengoff Street, Tel Aviv's main boulevard.

While the establishment of the state of Israel meant that the Zionists' dream of a Jewish state had come true, the Zionist myth of "a land without a people for a people without a land" was at odds with reality: The Jews' holy land was already inhabited by Palestinian Arabs. Two peoples tied their national identity to the same piece of land. What for the Israelis is the founding of their country—*Yom Ha'atzmaut*, "Independence Day"—is, for the Palestinians, *Nakba*—"The Catastrophe."

That same night, troops from five Arab countries—Egypt, Iraq, Transjordan, Lebanon, and Syria—marched into Israel with the proclaimed aim of destroying the newly declared state. Israel emerged as the winner of this first Arab-Israeli war, and with a considerably enlarged territory. The new borders included a much greater area than Israel had originally been granted by the United Nations. Around 700,000 Palestinians fled or were driven away; many Palestinian villages were destroyed.

This first war immediately following the founding of the state would be but one of many military disputes between Israel and its Arab neighbors.

Israel's history is inextricably tied to the history of the Palestinians; it is a succession of wars and terrorist attacks, of violence and counter-violence. It is impossible to recount it objectively, let alone in a few lines.

One reason why the Middle East conflict seems so intractable is that it is an entanglement of many different conflicts. It isn't just about the land. The Israeli historian Tom Segev writes: "The conflict is fueled not only by political, strategic, and economic interests, but also by fear and jealousy, faith and prejudice, myths and illusions."

Religious fanaticism, stoked by Muslim fundamentalists and ultra-Orthodox Jews, has long pervaded any dialogue on both sides.

Israel, the small country on the edge of the Mediterranean Sea with a current population of eight million people, cannot find peace: Externally, Israel is struggling with its Arab neighbors; internally, with itself. There is no peace between Israelis and Palestinians—but there is no peace between the deeply religious and the secular Jews either.

The deeply religious Orthodox Jews and modern, liberal Israelis are engaged in a bitter struggle for the prerogative of interpreting many political issues: What role should religion play in politics? How to deal with the Palestinians? Should the ultra-Orthodox settlers withdraw from the occupied territories, or should they remain and continue expanding their settlements under the constant guard of young Israeli snipers?

When Jennifer Teege arrived in Tel Aviv in late 1991, the city was already regarded as a haven for modern, democratic Israelis.

Tel Aviv has always been the center of the country's creative scene: Artists and writers come to live here; record labels, advertising agencies, and computer firms are headquartered here. Lefties and liberals, gays and lesbians love the city for its unorthodox way of life.

In the years after the creation of the state, so many Jews came to Tel Aviv that most of its dwellings were raised with lightning speed. Previously, young European architects had designed and constructed around 4,000 Bauhaus-style buildings here and thus created the "White City." Today, Tel Aviv is home to around 400,000 people, originating from over 100 different countries.

Tel Aviv is a place for new beginnings, a city without memories. It is a counter-world to the capital, Jerusalem, where every stone tells a story and religious fanaticism is rife.

Tel Aviv is young and modern, noisy and hectic, open-minded and tolerant. But it is not beautiful and picturesque like Jerusalem. In the summer, the stench of exhaust fumes and trash hangs over the city, and scrawny cats forage for food on the beach.

Israelis say that the most important word for living in the city is *lizrom*—be spontaneous, go with the flow. Jerusalem is the place for praying, they say, Haifa for working, and Tel Aviv for living.

Especially in the nineties, the city cultivated its image as the cool and buoyant party capital. It was often referred to as "the Bubble" thanks to the carefree attitude that prevailed on Tel Aviv's creative scene—despite the fact that the first intifada had begun in 1987, the same year that Palestinians in Gaza established the radical Islamist organization Hamas. Bombs were already exploding around the nation on a regular basis.

In early 1991, during the Gulf War, the Iraqi dictator Saddam Hussein repeatedly fired rockets at Tel Aviv and Haifa, although Israel was not officially involved in the conflict. Jennifer's friend Noa recalls: "During the Iraqi attacks we lived in constant fear for our lives. The sirens wailed again and again, announcing new attacks. For over two months I had plastic sheets taped around my windows to make them airtight. We had gas masks at the ready and enough stockpiled mineral water to last for weeks."

The Iraqi attacks ended almost a year before Jennifer Teege arrived in Tel Aviv. Noa says: "We had been through terrible times, so we were enjoying life even more. It was a carefree time, the most playful time I remember." At Tel Aviv's parties, suffering and danger seemed but a distant notion.

■　　■　　■

THE NEXT DAY I WAS UP EARLY. So far I had seen Tel Aviv only through the windows of a taxicab; now I wanted to explore the city on foot. I went to a café and ordered what I believed to be a typical Israeli breakfast: freshly squeezed orange juice and a bagel.

After breakfast I walked to the Tayelet, the seaside promenade,

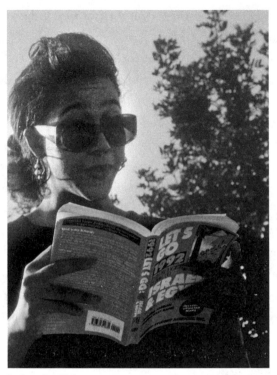

In Israel, 1992

where tall hotel towers line the seafront. Noa, who couldn't come with me because she had a lecture to attend, had suggested a must-do: "Get a view of the city from above!"

I stole into a four-star hotel on the beachfront and took the elevator to the top floor. The view was spectacular: On one side I could see Tel Aviv stretched out in front of me, from the skyscrapers in the center all the way to the suburbs. On the other side was the beach and then the sea.

I went down to the sea. Beachgoers with wet hair were walking around; joggers were running along the water's edge. Israeli pop music was playing in the beach cafés. Children were building sandcastles; surfers were paddling in the waves. I took my shoes off and dropped onto the hot sand.

Later I joined the crowds at Carmel Market, where stall-holders were hawking their wares: fruit and vegetables, underwear, fake Rolex watches. Opposite the market lies Shenkin Street, which, according to Noa, was the trendiest street in the Middle East: cafés and boutiques, records and designer clothing. The way back to Noa's apartment took me via Rothchild Boulevard, an impressive avenue where people of all ages gathered to play *boules* and talk about politics.

I wanted to explore every corner of this country and get to know its people. I was particularly looking forward to seeing Jerusalem: the golden cupola of the Dome of the Rock, the gleaming silver one of the Al-Aqsa Mosque. So far, all I knew about the city I had learned from books and stories; now I was going to see it with my own eyes. At Tel Aviv's Central Bus Station I boarded a *sherut*—a shared taxi—and headed for Jerusalem.

Through the dirty minibus windows I was barely able to make out the blurred landscape: bare hills interspersed with little villages, and every so often soldiers and military roadblocks. Tel Aviv is only 45 miles north of the Gaza Strip, and 35 miles west of the West Bank. I realized how small Israel is—much smaller than I had expected.

An hour later, we reached Jerusalem.

The bus let us off just a few meters outside the Damascus Gate at the northern side of the old city wall. I stopped in front of the massive archway. Armed soldiers with machine guns, helmets, and bulletproof vests were patrolling the battlements. When the soldiers noticed me looking at them, they fixed their gaze on me. I quickly turned away and hurried through the gate into the Old

City's Arab quarter: tight little alleyways, narrow townhouses, arcade shops. The air was scented with tea and herbs. Shopkeepers approached me, trying to entice me in. Children in blue school uniforms capered between the shops, and small traders pushing handcarts laden with fresh fruit and vegetables had to constantly stop and brake wherever the narrow alleyways became too steep.

I didn't see any Orthodox Jews in the Arab quarter of the Old City. Here, the Muslims generally lived among themselves. In the vicinity of the Wailing Wall, further east, it was a completely different picture: Devout Jews were rushing through the streets. They were wearing black trousers and long overcoats, their prayer tassels trailing below.

At the Wailing Wall, I was surprised to see people walking backward. Later I learned that they consider it disrespectful to turn their backs on the Temple and only turn around after they've backed away a few meters.

Men and women pray separately at the Wall. The men had donned their black-and-white prayer shawls and were reciting their prayers while swaying forward and back. Next to them were the women, at a smaller area of the Wall reserved for them. Their lips were moving silently in prayer.

I joined the women and touched the smooth, worn limestone with my hands. It is a Jewish tradition to insert messages and prayers into the cracks between the stones. Without thinking, I wrote a quick wish and squeezed it in with all the others between two stones of the Wall. Slowly I backed away. I had written that I wished for a boyfriend.

Jerusalem, the Holy City. A city sacred to three world religions and therefore fiercely contested like no other.

Here, Muslim, Christian, and Jewish pilgrimage destinations lie side by side: After Mecca and Medina, the Al-Aqsa Mosque and the Dome of the Rock are the Muslims' most important shrines; Christians pilgrimage to the Church of the Holy Sepulchre, where according to tradition Jesus was crucified and buried; and the Wailing Wall, the last remaining wall of the Second Temple, is the most sacred site recognized by the Jewish faith.

To whom does Jerusalem belong? The question has been one of the key issues since the beginning of the Middle East conflict. Jerusalem's legal status is unclear. From a practical point of view, the city is divided into a predominantly Arab eastern part and a Jewish western part.

But it is also divided between the deeply religious and the secular. Almost half of all strictly Orthodox Israelis—known as *Haredim*—live in Jerusalem. Their quarter, Mea Shearim, is reminiscent of a nineteenth century shtetl. The residents converse in Yiddish, a dialect based on medieval Middle High German. German speakers can understand it to an extent.

Haredi Jews believe in the strict separation of men and women in public. On buses, for example, women have to travel at the back. Many also oppose the secular state of Israel; they study the Torah and don't work. Around sixty percent of Haredi families in Israel are living in poverty.

Strictly Orthodox Jews often have very large families. Secular Israelis worry about the fact that in many Jerusalem schools, Orthodox Jewish children are in the majority. The influence Orthodox Jews have on Israeli politics is steadily growing.

MEA SHEARIM MEANS "City of a Hundred Gates." Noa and Anat had told me about this quarter of the religious Jews. They said that secular Israelis would avoid the area, and that on Shabbat, the weekly day of rest when observant Jews refrain from work activities, Mea Shearim residents would sometimes throw stones at strange cars approaching the area.

I wanted to see how the people there lived. I walked past derelict buildings and labyrinths of courtyards. Laundry strung across balconies was flapping in the wind.

The Old City of Jerusalem had a certain museum-like quality about it, an air of days gone by, but at the same time it was colorful and vibrant. Mea Shearim, however, felt dark and forbidding. The dwellings were built closely together. There were many children here, too, but they averted their eyes when they saw me looking at them.

The men wore hats or fur caps on their heads, their sidelocks curling down underneath.

The women wore ankle-length skirts and sandals with dark stockings. At first I wondered why all the women had the same pageboy haircut; then I remembered what Noa had told me: Orthodox women usually marry very young; subsequently they shave their heads and wear wigs in public.

At every other crossroads in Mea Shearim there were signs in various languages warning tourists not to enter the area with bare arms or legs.

The people in Mea Shearim live without radio, TV, or Internet. Instead, posters are plastered to the walls of the narrow townhouses, announcing the local news to the residents: the opening of new shops, public lectures, weddings. And some unusual messages: The rabbis were inviting the community to pray for rain, next to a warning that boys and girls are not allowed to walk through the district together.

How could they live like that, in a world full of commands and prohibitions, thrown back to the nineteenth century?

Noa had told me about a friend of hers who married an Orthodox man. Noa was very sad about it: "She lives on a different planet now."

I took a sherut back to Tel Aviv. It was late when I arrived. There were only a few people in the streets. It was Friday night—Shabbat had begun. Candles were burning in the windows of many apartments; families were setting the dinner table together.

Noa and Anat didn't celebrate Shabbat. We sat talking together for a long time that night. I wanted to know more about their country. Anat suggested I join a kibbutz for a while and work alongside volunteers from all over the world for free board and lodging. During her military service, she had lived on Kibbutz Eilot in the south of Israel, where she met her boyfriend, Alon. The next morning, Anat called the kibbutz and arranged a place for me.

■　■　■

Anat's partner, Alon, grew up on Eilot. A few weeks after his birth in 1965, his parents took him to the children's house at the kibbutz. There, he lived with the other children, cared for by nurses and teachers. He saw his mother every afternoon before returning to the children's house for bedtime. He still remembers how much he missed his mother at night.

In the early years of many kibbutzim, the patriarchal nuclear family—father, mother, children—seemed like an outdated model. Instead, the task of raising the children was delegated to nurses and teachers. Women were expected to work, just like the men. Housework was centralized, too: The kibbutzim had communal laundries, tailor shops, kitchens, and dining halls where everyone ate together.

The central idea behind the kibbutzim is collective living. The founders of the first kibbutzim were inspired by socialist and Zionist ideas. They wanted to create a socialist Jewish state on their own soil.

The first kibbutz was founded on the shores of the Sea of Galilee, over a hundred years ago. In 2014, there were around 270 of these villages all over Israel.

Kibbutz Eilot was founded in 1962. It lies at the southern tip of Israel, on the edge of the Negev desert, surrounded by rugged mountain ranges, between Jordan and Egypt.

Israeli writer Amos Oz spent 25 years living on a kibbutz. In sum, he says: "The founders hoped to change more than just the social system, the class society. They wanted to revolutionize human nature. They believed that if they created a society where everyone ate the same, dressed the same, worked the same, and shared the same living standard, all selfishness would disappear and a new human being would arise. That turned out not to be the case."

When Alon finished school, he did not receive any vocational training or academic education. He took it for granted that he would work in the workshops on the kibbutz.

■　■　■

I CAUGHT A BUS THAT SET off for the south. After three hours' journey the driver stopped, in the middle of the desert. All around me there was nothing but red dust and rocks. I marched up the road and found the kibbutz on a hill. At first glance it looked like a holiday complex: identical, two-story buildings separated by green lawns, flagstone paths, and rampant oleander bushes.

The workday began at six a.m. I had hoped to help milk the cows; I thought that might be more exciting than, say, sorting tomatoes on a conveyor belt. It was not to be. On the first morning, I was sent to the kitchen. My job for the day was to dispose of leftovers and to pre-rinse the dirty dishes. On day two, I was moved to the dishwasher. Loading vast numbers of dirty plates into the machine was incredibly tedious, and I wondered if this was really the best way to get a more in-depth picture of Israel.

The next day, I packed my bags and left.

I traveled a few miles further to Israel's southernmost city, the beach resort of Eilat by the Red Sea. Looking to boost my travel funds, I headed to the port, an alleged insider's tip amongst penniless backpackers. A large sailing yacht was just putting out to sea. I ran along the pier and shouted to one of the crew: "Are you looking for some help?" "Sorry, we are full!" he shouted back.

Then I saw a wide, red boat enter the harbor, with a tall, dark, and lean man at the helm. When the last passenger had disembarked, I approached the captain: "Hi, do you need some help?" He smiled: "Yes, someone left this morning."

His name was Shimon, and I fell in love instantly. He had a weather-beaten face with bright blue eyes under heavy eyebrows. Shimon was a Sabra—the term for native Israeli Jews, after the Hebrew name for the prickly pear: hard and spiky on the outside, but soft and sweet on the inside.

Shimon was forty-eight and married with a young daughter. He had spent half his life serving in the Israeli Defense Force, including in Shayetet 13, the elite unit of the Israeli Navy. He had moved to Eilat a few years earlier, and now made his living by operating a glass-bottomed boat between Eilat and the Egyptian border.

I became a member of the crew, together with two other backpackers, a Dutch girl and a South African man. During the day, I would sell tickets to tourists; in the evenings I'd scrub the deck and the toilets. At night, I would fetch my camping mat, unroll my sleeping bag, and find a place to sleep on the boat, under the open sky.

Shimon and I came from different worlds, but we had things in common: We both enjoyed our own company, and we loved tranquility. Shimon took me on a trip to the Negev desert. I had never been to the desert before, but I loved it straight away. It may appear bleak at first—a vast, barren emptiness. But there is so much to discover in the barrenness. We walked through narrow gorges. Shimon showed me unusual rock formations and pointed out how the color of the rock changes over the course of the day. We discovered plants in the desert, and saw snakes and scorpions.

At first it didn't bother me that Shimon didn't talk much. I could have walked through the desert with him in silence for days.

For the first time, someone loved me for who I was.

After a few weeks, however, my usual restlessness kicked in. Did our relationship have a future, or was I wasting my time in Eilat? Shimon didn't understand what I was worried about. True, he was still living with his wife, he said, but the marriage was long finished. He asked: "Why don't you just stay here?" He suggested we move in together in Eilat.

I asked for some time to consider and flew back to Germany. My tourist visa was only valid for three months and about to expire. Back home in Munich, my adoptive parents didn't push me or ask when I might start college. They must have known that I didn't feel like talking. My friends, on the other hand, spoke quite bluntly: They asked me what I, at twenty-one, wanted with such an old man, and suggested I was looking for a father figure.

I did some temp work with Siemens to earn some money. Then I flew back to Eilat.

Shimon's wife had moved out of the apartment, leaving their daughter with us. She was four years old, a beautiful little girl with long, dark curls that had a tendency to fall over her eyes. In the mornings, she went to preschool; in the afternoons, she was either with me or with her mother.

Shimon worked on the boat. I wished for more independence; I wanted to earn my own money. I had a job waiting for me at the holiday club Méditerranée in Eilat, but the season had not yet started. In the meantime I was supposed to be learning Hebrew, but after five minutes I would usually put my books to one side and stroll over to the beach or to the nearby shopping mall.

In the evenings, when Shimon came home, his daughter would leap up and fling her arms around his neck. She came first. He would play with her and read her long stories before putting her to bed. Afterward he would collapse, exhausted, on the sofa. I felt abandoned. This was not how I had imagined my life with Shimon.

One evening, after I had been sitting on the sofa waiting for him yet again, it all came bursting out. I assailed him with grievances, complaining that his life revolved around his daughter and adding that I had cheated on him with an old boyfriend during my recent stay in Germany.

Shimon looked at me calmly. He said that his behavior wasn't the problem, nor was his daughter. "You don't know what you want. Why are you wrecking everything?" Then he leaned back. An oppressive silence hung in the air.

Sometimes I think that if I had met Shimon at a later point in my life, we might have had a future. But at the time, I was too young. I was looking for a savior, not a partner. It was asking too much.

The next morning, I packed my bags and went back to Tel Aviv. I had called Noa in the night after my argument with Shimon.

Shimon didn't contact me. After five days, I went to a travel agent and booked a flight to Germany for the next morning. That night, I set the alarm for 4:30 a.m.

Warm sunlight was falling on my face as I woke up. I squinted. I could see the packed bag by my bed; I could hear banging in the kitchen. I got up and stuck my head out the door. Noa was at the stove and gave me a cheery wave. After we had breakfast together, I went to a language school for newly arrived immigrants and signed up for a Hebrew class.

■ ■ ■

Noa remembers how Jennifer arrived crying, with her bags at her feet, at her door in Tel Aviv: "She was so in love with Shimon, and so desperate."

When Jennifer's alarm went off on the day of her planned departure, Noa tried to get her out of bed, "but Jenny just mumbled that she was tired and rolled over."

It still makes Noa laugh to think about that morning: "She overslept once—and stayed for four years!" Jennifer was vivacious and spontaneous, Noa says about her friend. "Jenny used to make up her own Hebrew words—we laughed so much."

Jennifer was a great friend, both for having fun with and for meaningful conversations: "When I first met her in Paris, we felt very close very quickly. Our friendship is one of the most extraordinary friendships I've ever had, full of wonderful times and crazy coincidences. I always tell her it was a godsend that she missed that flight."

■ ■ ■

HEBREW IS A SEMITIC LANGUAGE. Unlike with English or French, it was impossible for me to deduce the meanings of new words by myself. My teacher at the Ulpan, the language school for newly arrived immigrants, made every effort. She was able to explain new words using gestures and facial expressions. If someone didn't understand the expression for "to lie down," she lay down on the desk. It didn't take long for me to be able to follow simple conversations. But it was a long time before I had the courage to speak in Hebrew. Time and again I became exasperated by this new language and its complicated grammar.

I found my own place to live. I met Tzahi, an actor, and we rented a three-bedroom apartment on Engel Street together. At the time, Tzahi was not yet the successful actor he was to become, but he was very popular with women. He was in his mid-thirties, blond, bright, and handsome. Many people thought that we were together, but Tzahi was like a brother to me. We often cooked together or played "guess the capital" while we were doing the dishes. Our roommates changed often, but he and I remained the solid core.

Once I had finished my language course, I applied to study at Tel Aviv University for a degree in Middle Eastern studies and African studies. When the acceptance letter landed in my mailbox, it took a huge weight off my mind. Up to that point, my future had been uncertain. Now I knew—I was going to college in Israel!

In the lectures I sat among Israelis. The lecturers spoke Hebrew, so at first I hardly understood anything at all and spent a lot of time reading up on the topics. I was allowed to take the exams in English. For my Middle Eastern classes I learned Arabic and translated parts of the Koran. Often I would stay up until midnight, my head bent over a book at my poorly lit desk.

I had a new boyfriend, Elias. He had been sitting behind me in one of my Arabic classes and kept staring at me. When we talked during the break, we hit it off straight away. I soon gave him the key to my apartment. I tried to forget about Shimon, but I couldn't.

In the little spare time I had outside my studies, I often met with Noa and Anat. I had become close friends with Anat, too. She was just there, in her quiet, caring way. I once went on a trip to the Sinai Peninsula where I drank tea with the Bedouins in the desert and contracted a bad infection. Back in Israel, I was hospitalized for several days. When I was discharged, I was still weak and feverish. Anat would come and sit by my bedside—and she spent hours in the kitchen making me chicken soup.

I admire Anat for her modest, unpretentious way of living. She eventually moved in with her boyfriend Alon on the kibbutz near Eilat, where I had only stuck it out for a couple of days. Today, Anat works as a nurse; I can't imagine a better profession for her.

■   ■   ■

Anat describes how she spent many hours with Jennifer, walking through Tel Aviv: "We would talk—about Israeli politics or Israeli men. I usually put on my platform shoes because I'm so short and Jennifer is so tall. We stood out when we went out together." Anat also recalls that Jennifer would often be approached by strangers when they walked on the beach: "Some people wanted to know whether Jennifer was a professional basketball player. Or model scouts would come up to her and want to book her for some photo shoot or other. But she always replied, 'No, I am studying.' She was never one of those naïve, clueless girls. She was very independent and seemed to know what she wanted. Friends would often come to her with their problems and ask her for advice."

■ ■ ■

I SPENT A LOT OF MY TIME at the Goethe Institute in Tel Aviv. It was before the days when German newspapers were available on the Internet. I borrowed piles of books, and read literature about the Holocaust, Zionism, and the Middle East conflict. Soon I was known by everyone at the institute, and ultimately I was offered a part-time job in the library. From then on I would go to work there in the mornings and to college in the afternoons.

The Goethe Institute mostly attracted young Israelis who came there to learn German. But older Israelis came, too: Holocaust survivors who wanted to read and hear the German language again. They didn't talk about what they had gone through, but I saw the tattooed numbers on their arms. Initially, I was quite self-conscious and felt that I had to apologize for being German.

The color of my skin was good camouflage: Most visitors to the institute assumed that I was American or maybe one of the many Ethiopian Jews who were arriving in Israel at the time. But once I opened my mouth and started speaking in fluent German, they knew. When I mentioned that I was German to my fellow students at college, they looked at me in amazement: How could

I be from Germany? they wanted to know. How did I end up there?

Some of the Holocaust survivors who came to the Goethe Institute had failing eyesight. If I had the time, I would sit down with them and read German newspapers and novels aloud.

Much later, when I discovered my family history, I was glad that I had read to the old people then. I hadn't done it because I felt guilty, but just because I wanted to. At the time, I had no idea that my grandfather had murdered people just like them.

Two elderly ladies came regularly. They asked about my studies, and we talked about everyday issues. I didn't dare ask them about their history. I just spoke with them in German and told them about today's Germany—so different from the one that they had known.

Once, at an event held at the Goethe Institute, I was talking with a sixteen-year-old Israeli boy who told me that he had been learning German at school for the past three years. I praised his pronunciation. And then, out of the blue, he said that almost his entire family had died in concentration camps. I was ashamed and didn't know what to say, but eventually I blurted out: "Well, what really counts is that you and I can be here together now and talk."

I think he noticed my embarrassment. In any case, he smiled at me and asked if I had ever been to Berlin, or if I had heard of the German punk rock band Die Toten Hosen.

The abrupt change of topic seemed bizarre, but at the same time it was characteristic of that generation of young Israelis. To them, Germany was both the Nazis and the present. They asked me about Boris Becker, Helmut Kohl, and reunification. It hadn't been long since the Berlin Wall came down.

· · ·

Nathan Durst is a psychologist and deputy chairman of AMCHA, the Israeli center providing assistance and counseling to Holocaust survivors and their families. He sees differences between second- and third-generation descendants of victims of the Holocaust.

Most of the children would have grown up with their parents' silence on the subject, he says: "Some of them would have been named after a murdered relative; yet many parents would not talk to their children about their experiences—because they didn't want to relive the horrors, but also because they were ashamed of the humiliation that they had suffered." But the children could still sense that their parents had gone through terrible ordeals, he adds, speculating that this may be why the second generation still struggles to entertain the idea of reconciliation. "The children of survivors often did not want to have anything to do with Germans. They felt hatred and wanted revenge."

According to Durst, the third generation regards Germans in a different light, clearly differentiating between the past and the present. "Often it is their grandchildren that the victims open up to about their time in the concentration camps, about the experiences that they had locked up inside for so long. It has a healing effect on the whole family: Once things are out in the open and being talked about, they can usually be dealt with much more easily."

· · ·

EACH YEAR IN THE SPRING, Israel observes Holocaust Remembrance Day. Sirens wail all over the country; for two minutes everything stops, and people remember the victims of the Holocaust. I always found these two minutes very moving, the silent reflection very powerful. I would stand there, among the Israelis, and feel that I was part of the Jewish community of mourners.

With my Israeli friends of my own age, my nationality and the past were irrelevant: Noa and I talked about everyday life, about college. Our friendship thrived on frivolity and the typical things twenty-year-olds care about, such as betting on which of his many female admirers my handsome roommate Tzahi would take to bed next.

During the early days of my stay in Israel, I devoted myself to learning everything there was to know about the Holocaust. Later, the here and now came to the fore. While I was in Israel, apartheid was abolished in South Africa. Since I was also taking African studies at college, this was an important subject for me.

In Middle Eastern studies, we looked into the different conflicts in the Middle East. Unlike my fellow students, I often traveled to the occupied territories, to the West Bank and the Gaza Strip. Hearing about the Palestinians' lives from my Israeli lecturers wasn't enough for me; I wanted to talk with the people living there in order to gauge their situation realistically.

The first time I went to Gaza, I went with a friend who worked for a Palestinian aid organization. I remember how shocked I was when I saw the squalid and derelict homes and streets in Gaza. Posters with PLO Chairman Yasser Arafat's face where everywhere.

The situation in the refugee camps was unbearable. People who had fled their homes decades ago were still living in temporary accommodations. Children were gamboling around the tents, but I didn't see any playgrounds or parks, only dust and desperation. The Palestinians I spoke with kept saying, "Life and death are in Allah's hands." I didn't ask who was to blame, but I couldn't forget the suffering of the people there.

During the four years that I lived in Israel, the political situation escalated. One morning I was waiting at my bus stop in Tel Aviv, part of my daily commute to the Goethe Institute. A line 5 bus arrived; the waiting passengers got on. Shortly afterward, I boarded a different bus. When I reached the Goethe Institute twenty minutes later, I knew straight away that something bad must have happened. The institute is right next to the Ichilov Hospital, and ambulances were speeding past me, sirens wailing and blue lights flashing. Inside the institute, my colleagues were already standing in front of the TV, watching the breaking news. A suicide bomber had blown up the line 5 bus in the center of Tel Aviv. The pictures showed pools of blood and the obliterated bus.

I had taken that bus on numerous occasions. I suddenly realized that I could lose my life in this country that wasn't my own.

■　■　■

The suicide attack on the line 5 bus on Dizengoff Street in October 1994 marked the arrival of political violence in Tel Aviv. The bombing shook the city that represented a modern Israel. Twenty-two people died; forty-eight were injured.

It was the first major attack carried out by the radical Islamist group Hamas since the signing of the Oslo Accords in 1993 and 1994, when Israeli Prime Minister Yitzhak Rabin and Yasser Arafat, chairman of the PLO, had agreed on the withdrawal of the Israeli Defense Forces from parts of the West Bank and the Gaza Strip. The agreements provided for the creation of Palestinian self-government and the renunciation of violence. However, particularly contentious issues, such as the question of the Jewish settlements in Israeli-occupied territories, the status of Jerusalem, and the return of Palestinian refugees, were deliberately kept out of the agreement to be decided at a later stage.

In 1994, Rabin, Arafat, and Israel's then-minister of defense, Shimon Peres, were awarded the Nobel Peace Prize. In a later speech, Yitzhak Rabin promised to "end, once and for all, a hundred years of bloodshed."

Rabin was severely criticized for his policies by the radical Israeli right, while the Islamist organizations Hamas and Palestine Islamic Jihad attempted to disrupt the peace process with terrorist attacks.

On November 4, 1995, Yitzhak Rabin was assassinated at a peace rally by Jigal Amir, an Israeli right-wing extremist.

The bombing of that packed Israeli bus was not the last; many more were to follow. From then on, no one in Tel Aviv or anywhere in Israel could board a bus, or visit a café, bar, or shopping mall, without fearing an attack.

When Yitzak Rabin died, hope for peace in the Middle East died with him.

■　■　■

I HADN'T ANTICIPATED THE ATTACK on Yitzhak Rabin. The country was in mourning. An Israeli had killed another Israeli. The danger hadn't come from the outside—not from Gaza, the West Bank, or Lebanon—but from within Israel's own ranks. Rabin's assassination revealed how disjointed the country was.

My view of Israel had been changing for some time: My initial euphoria had been replaced with a deep skepticism. I was living in a highly armed country, surrounded by hostile neighbors. I was aware now of the serious threat that the country was facing, the intractable conflict it was engaged in. And of how one's view of the world became very one-sided for those that lived here.

I can't say exactly when the depressions began. All I know is that I found myself walking through Tel Aviv on my own. No longer happy and outgoing, but sad and introverted. I felt no joy and no curiosity. It was as if a wall had appeared between me and my surroundings.

When I breathed in, I didn't get enough air. I felt like I was being choked.

I grew more and more withdrawn; I wanted to be on my own. I only left the house if I absolutely had to, to go to work or to the library for my studies. I didn't discuss my worries with Noa or Anat; I would not have been able to explain the state I was in.

What was wrong with me? I could find no obvious reason for my sadness. I wasn't homesick; I received regular visits from my friends and my adoptive family. My degree program had been the right choice, too—at last I was doing something that I was really interested in.

No matter how hard I thought about it, there was no explanation for my unhappy state of mind. I scolded myself for being ungrateful. I had seen how people lived in the Palestinian refugee camps. I, on the other hand, was living the good life; I had all I could possibly need. Why couldn't I appreciate that? Why did I find everything so hard?

Perhaps, I thought, the reasons for my sadness could not be found in the present. Perhaps they dated back to something in the past.

I barely managed to concentrate on my final exams. The harder I crammed, the less I seemed to remember.

Jennifer's adoptive family came to visit her during that time. Her brother Matthias was shocked when he saw her: "Jenny was completely exhausted. I was alarmed by her lifestyle: She had thrown herself fully into her studies, obsessing about details with an exaggerated intensity—as if she wanted to prove something to us." Matthias had the impression that Jennifer wanted to demonstrate to her adoptive family what she was now capable of: "As if her worthiness depended on her being the best."

Noa and Anat also noticed that Jennifer wasn't well, but she didn't want any help. Noa says: "We were really close friends, but Jenny still liked to sort out her problems by herself."

•   •   •

SOMEHOW I MANAGED TO PASS my final exams. Afterward, I invited Noa, Anat, and a couple of other friends over for dinner. The following morning, I left Israel.

I went back to Munich and started therapy. I took a part-time editorial job with Bayerische Fernsehen, the Bavarian television network. Shortly after my twenty-seventh birthday, I suffered a nervous breakdown—during a conversation with my boss, I started to cry and couldn't stop.

I spent the following days in bed, the duvet pulled over my head. When a friend of mine called, I picked up the receiver and told her to call me back in six months. I didn't want to see anyone, only to stay in bed and sleep.

People who have never suffered from depression cannot imagine what it's like to be depressed. They may assume that depression is like an ordinary emotional low: For a while you "don't feel so good," but at some point you'll start to feel better.

I didn't start to feel better. I fell into a deep hole. My breathlessness became more and more frightening; I was gasping for air and thought I was going to die. When I was at my worst, I would have preferred to die. I never seriously considered taking my own life, but I hoped that I might cross a road and get run over by a car, so that everything would be over.

I had applied for a postgraduate course at the London School of Economics and been offered a place, but there was no way that I could accept it in my current condition. Instead of going to university in London, I went to therapy three times a week.

The first kind of therapy I tried was classic psychoanalysis. I lay on the couch and talked about what was going on in my life or what was on my mind at the time. Often I would talk about things from my past or about my dreams.

During the many hours I spent with my Munich therapist, the subject of my mother resurfaced. My underlying feelings of being given away and abandoned had not been resolved, but merely suppressed. I also suddenly discovered an interest in who my father was.

At elementary school, the other children had always wanted to know where I was from and why my skin was so dark. I would tell them that my father was an African chief who rode through the jungle on elephant-back. Later, I would claim that my father was Idi Amin, the cruel dictator who controlled Uganda in the seventies. He was the only African ruler I knew of as a child. I thought it would make the other children understand that I didn't want to talk about the subject and that they would leave me in peace.

When I moved to Paris after my high school graduation, I spent days wandering through the streets of Goutte d'Or, the African neighborhood in Paris's 18th arrondissement. At the market, stall-holders sold sweet potatoes and cassava roots next to smoked pikes that looked like shriveled rubber. Street vendors offered roasted peanuts and corn on the cob. The women, dressed in brightly patterned, tie-dyed wraps, carried their children on their backs and their shopping on their heads. At the hairdresser's, women would have their long hair braided. One of the market stalls flew a Togolese flag.

Africa suddenly seemed very near.

It was a strange world to me, but at the same time I had a sense of homecoming. I liked the beat of the African music and the kaleidoscope of colors. Here, finally, people didn't look back at me over their shoulders or stare at me from the corner of their eyes.

In Germany, black people are a minority. When we run into each other on the street, we nod and say "hello" even if we don't know one another. Our skin color creates an affinity.

In the African quarter of Paris, the color of my skin was nothing out of the ordinary. For the first time in my life, I felt that I was among my own kind.

I inherited my dark skin from my father. *Where was he now?* I wondered. Who was he? And who was I?

I decided to find my father, and so I contacted CPS. He was living in a village in Germany.

I sent him a little note to find out if he wanted to see me. A few days later I received his reply, on lime-green stationery, in ornate handwriting and polished German. He thanked me for my letter and said that he had always hoped, and even expected, to hear from me one day. Now a huge weight had been lifted from his mind. He would be excited to meet me, he added, and was looking forward to getting to know me at last, to catching up on everything he had missed out on over all these years.

We arranged to meet in a restaurant. When he arrived, he presented me with a rose.

My father is Nigerian. He told me that he was from Umutu, a small town in the southeast of Nigeria, and that he belonged to the Igbo people, an ethnic group in Nigeria. Originally forest farmers, today they are predominantly traders, craftsmen, and civil servants. The majority of the Igbo belong to the Christian faith.

My father told me that, when he set off for Germany in the late sixties, he was one of the first people to leave his village. At the time, anyone in Nigeria who aspired to a career sought a Western education. Besides, the country was ravaged by civil war.

After he studied in Germany, my father returned to Nigeria, where he worked for the government. He explained how the corruption drove him to despair: Computers designated for schools ended up with employees of the ministry. Eventually he moved back to Germany. Today, he is married to a German woman and has five other children. My half-siblings.

When I was born, he wanted me to be brought up by my African grandmother in Umutu. I learn that my father gave me an African name, Isioma, a traditional Igbo name meaning "Lucky."

My father gave me two books by the Nigerian writer Chinua Achebe, which I enjoyed very much. The books are about African traditions and about a kind of personal god that the Igbo people believe in: the *chi* that determines one's life. When a person loses their way, their chi will try to lead him back to the right path, Achebe explains.

I, too, wonder if life is just a succession of coincidences, or if we are guided by some higher power like chi. For a long time I didn't believe in fate, only in chance. But since I learned about my family history, I have thought differently. We are not free in our decisions—some things about our journey through life are predetermined.

After our meal at the restaurant, we went our separate ways: My father returned to his family, and I went back to Munich, to my old life.

As a child, I had known my mother, and so I missed her. My father, on the other hand, had always been a stranger to me. I had been curious about him and wanted to meet him in order to understand more about myself. But I had never felt a longing for him. Our meeting didn't change my feelings for him, either. He remained a stranger to me.

I saw him once more, when he invited me to his home. I met his family, his wife and children. I could see that my father was making every effort, but I was overwhelmed by all these new people. We said a cordial good-bye. I didn't see him again for a long time.

A few months later I moved to Hamburg. A friend had told me about a new media agency there. I wanted to get away from the heaviness of the political issues at the television network. I thought a job in advertising would be more lighthearted. By then, I felt emotionally strong enough to hold down a regular job.

■ ■ ■

The photo Jennifer Teege included with her application for the job in Hamburg shows her wearing a summer top and massive sunglasses. She also sent in a number of ideas for TV and magazine ads, as well as her report card from first grade: "Jennifer has integrated well into the class."

Her application suited the agency, and it suited the times. In the late nineties, the new economy was still booming. The agency was hiring new people every month; there was plenty to do. Hairdressers and masseurs would come to the office; in the mornings there was breakfast for all. The workday started at 9 a.m., and if you went home at 6 p.m., your colleagues in the open-plan office would ask: "Just doing a half-day today?"

■   ■   ■

ON MY FIRST DAY AT THE NEW JOB, a tall man with a deep voice approached me in the corridor: "Are you new here?" He was the agency boss. Goetz. The man I would go on to share my life with.

Newly in love, I would sit in a top-floor office in the center of Hamburg, writing copy for online marketing campaigns for banks and tobacco, car and furniture brands.

I enjoyed my work. The atmosphere was good, everybody was in high spirits. The campaigns for such a diverse range of products gave me the perfect excuse to act out my curiosity at last. I have always quizzed the people around me; I'm interested in how other people live—from where they go on vacation to what sort of bed they sleep in, what kind of sofa they sit on.

But it didn't take long for the same old problems to raise their heads again. It turned out that I still didn't have a grip on my depression. It was no longer a constant issue, but it came in bouts. At some point, every new task would cause me to panic. I would spend days playing around with old texts in order to look busy. Once I pretended I had the flu to avoid having to go to work.

Telling the truth was not an option. The world of advertising is all about perfect façades. No one talks about mental health problems, since they are counterproductive to creativity. At the time, I felt under constant pressure. Once a week, I went to a psychological self-help group. On those evenings, I always skulked off early under some pretext.

■ ■ ■

Goetz Teege is a quiet, levelheaded man of few words. Regarding his wife, Jennifer, he says: "It was love at first sight. She inspires me." Goetz Teege comes from a stable family and has four siblings. He tries to relate to the kind of upbringing Jennifer had: "Her fundamental problem is that she has learned not to rely on anyone." Despite her difficult childhood, his wife has "enormous strength," he says. "I was always fascinated by that side of her: Whenever she was feeling low, she fought hard to get over it. She sought to understand, to get to the bottom of it. She always felt that there was something that she didn't know about. Something that she needed to find out in order to get a handle on her life."

■ ■ ■

MY RELATIONSHIP WITH GOETZ BECAME STEADY. Soon, we were talking about children. He was seven years older than I and already had two children from a previous marriage; he wasn't sure if he wanted to become a father again. If he had decided that he didn't want any more children, I would have ended our relationship. I could not imagine a life without children. At age 32, I gave birth to my first son; two years later I had my second.

I endeavored to give my sons all those things that I went without for years: warmth, security. Normality.

Today, the most important thing I want them to come away

with is a strong sense of self-worth. I don't want them to have to work as hard for it as I did, in hundreds of hours of therapy.

At first, I found it incredibly hard to leave the children with anyone. I didn't have the heart to say good-bye to them. Whenever the babysitter came, I would sneak out to spare them the pain of separation.

Today, I would do things differently. I have come to understand that children can tolerate a brief good-bye, a short separation. It is much worse to leave without saying good-bye at all: If children find their mother suddenly gone, it erodes their basic sense of trust.

■   ■   ■

Jennifer Teege's brother, Matthias, notices that his sister is a very tense and anxious kind of mother to her sons: "She is very protective of her children, maybe too protective."

Matthias believes that Jennifer demands too much of herself: "In Israel, she strove to be the perfect student. Now she aims to be the perfect mother." Jennifer's perception of the model mother is a mother who is there for her children 24/7, he explains. "She tries to offer them the kind of childhood she never had. She tries to be the mother she would have liked to have."

After her marriage to Goetz and the birth of her sons, Jennifer Teege's depression gave way to a more bearable sadness. Her life seemed secure—until the day, at age 38, she found the book about her mother.

Suddenly, Anat and Noa stopped hearing from their friend. Anat says: "We would normally be in regular contact, but then it just ended abruptly. For months, we didn't hear a word from Jennifer. Noa and I were really worried; we kept sending her emails: 'What's up with you? Please write to us!'"

■ ■ ■

AFTER I FOUND THE BOOK about my mother, I couldn't bring myself to write to Noa and Anat. I needed time to recover from the shock.

When I was ready to turn to my friends in Israel, I realized how hard it was. It felt as if I had led some kind of double life all these years. As if I had been lying to my friends and all the people around me.

Even though the family secret was not my fault, I had a guilty conscience. I was particularly scared of telling Noa; I didn't know how she would cope. Some things affected her deeply.

Had Noa lost any relatives during the Holocaust? We had discussed the subject during my studies in Israel. I knew that none of her close family members had been murdered, but I knew nothing of her more distant relations. Had anyone been killed at Płaszów? If she had mentioned it at the time, I might not have taken note.

I would have felt more comfortable telling my story to Anat; she is not unsettled so easily. But I needed to talk to Noa first.

And so I didn't confide in either of my friends, and I only answered their emails sporadically. We didn't see each other for nearly three years.

Every year at Rosh Hashanah, the Jewish New Year, Noa sent me photos of her family. Sometimes she would write to me on the occasion of other Jewish festivals, too, or for family events. I usually replied with just a few short sentences.

Finally, Noa announced that she was coming to the next Berlinale, Berlin's annual international film festival. Noa had become a screenwriter in Israel. Every time she came to the Berlinale, we would try to meet up; our reunions there had become a little ritual. I hadn't been in touch for a long time—if I didn't go to Berlin now, she would think that I was deliberately trying to avoid her.

But on the other hand, I couldn't go to the festival and talk with Noa about trivial matters. I couldn't and wouldn't lie to her if she asked what was up with me. We had known each other for too long for that.

The Berlinale was going to show a film for which Noa had written the screenplay; it was about an autistic boy. My old roommate Tzahi played one of the main characters.

I knew how long Noa had been working on this screenplay—for years. She was always talking about it. Now, she had invited me to Berlin; she wanted me to sit next to her when it was shown at the cinema. It would be her big moment—one I wanted to share with her, not destroy with my story.

I had once made the mistake of telling a good friend my family's story at a birthday party. My friend had become so upset that she couldn't enjoy the rest of the party.

I wrote a long email to Noa's husband Yoel and explained the difficult situation I found myself in: There was something on my mind that I needed to discuss with Noa, but I didn't want to tell her at the film festival. I wrote down the whole story and asked him to share it with Noa. I also asked him how many relatives he and Noa had lost in the Holocaust, and if anyone they knew had died in Płaszów.

Yoel wrote back: "We have all lost someone. The Holocaust is in our DNA, it is why we are here. But how is that your fault? The

Berlin film festival is a great moment for Noa, but you won't spoil it for her. She is longing to see you again, she's missing you. I am sure that she will listen to your story and help you however she can. You don't need to spare her. You need us to support and look after you now, not the other way round. Noa will always be your friend, in good times and bad."

■   ■   ■

Yoel and Noa are sitting in their apartment in the center of Tel Aviv as they tell their family stories.

Noa's father's family was living in the US when Hitler came to power; they were safe.

Noa's mother's family was from Poland and Russia. Her maternal grandmother was living in Stolin, Belarus, when the war broke out. She was deported to Siberia under Stalin. Her parents, her four siblings, and their children stayed behind and were killed by Germans in a massacre, along with hundreds of other Jews.

Relatives of Noa's maternal grandfather were killed in the ghetto of Pinsk in what was then Poland. His brother died in the Majdanek concentration camp, near Lublin.

Noa's husband, Yoel, also lost relatives in Poland. He recalls how in the seventies, when they were still children, he and his friends were surprised to learn that a neighbor owned a Volkswagen Beetle. This neighbor had been imprisoned in a concentration camp—and now he was driving a German car!

That was a long time ago, Yoel says. He laughs and points to his stove: Siemens!

In Yoel's hometown, there were couples who adopted children because they could not have children themselves: They had become infertile due to the abuse and medical experiments they had suffered in concentration camps. They were severely traumatized people, living in constant fear that their adoptive children would one day disappear or be taken away from them.

Yoel very carefully told his wife what he had learned from Jennifer's email. Noa says that she was shocked: "I had never been so intimate with a close relative of a Nazi criminal." Noa had other German friends, too, and wondered what crimes their grandfathers might have committed during the war.

Why had she never asked? "At first I didn't dare ask about their grandparents. And later the subject was so far removed. If you are friends with someone, you don't discuss whether their grandparents may have killed or informed on your grandparents. It's particularly striking in Jenny's case: Her and Amon Goeth—I just can't wrap my head around it!"

Noa is convinced: "It was fate that I met Jenny as a young woman. It would have been impossible to strike up a friendship if we had known that her grandfather was a concentration camp commandant. How could she have come up to me, with such a rucksack full of guilt? How could I have met her without any bias?"

It would have been so complicated, she adds—a tense, "reaching hands across the graves" sort of friendship.

Today, Noa explains, she can deal with Jennifer's story. She has known Jennifer for twenty years and sees her only as a friend, not as the granddaughter of a Nazi: "I told her, forget Amon Goeth. You are Jenny! Please, come!"

■   ■   ■

I AM BACK IN ISRAEL NOW, at Noa's. She has moved; I had to hunt for her new apartment. After we embrace and Noa shows me

Jennifer Teege and her friend Noa in a café in Tel Aviv

around, we sit in the sun on her patio, talking and watching the goings-on in the street below. It is like always, only better, since now there is nothing between us.

A few weeks ago I was sitting next to Noa in the dark, watching clips of her film at the Berlin film festival. It was just as I had hoped—sharing that significant moment in her life.

Now, in Tel Aviv, Noa's film is showing at the Dizengoff Center downtown. That evening, we go to see the full-length movie. It is called *Mabul (The Flood)*. We see Tzahi on screen, playing the father. I like the story; it's about a family with an autistic son. It shows how important it is to stick together and not give up, even in trying times.

After the movie, Noa and I go to a café. We talk about all the things we have done and been through together. We are closer than ever. There is nothing left to hide; everything feels good and right.

After a quick visit to Jerusalem, I travel to Eilat. To Anat. I had asked Noa to tell her everything.

■ ■ ■

Anat cried when she heard Jennifer's story.

This scene from *Schindler's List* instantly came to her mind: a man on his balcony, shooting people as a pastime. Jennifer's grandfather.

Anat switched the film off at the balcony scene. She couldn't bear it.

When Anat shows old, faded family photographs, she often explains, "he was shot," or "she was gassed."

Anat's mother's family was originally from Poland. Anat's great-grandparents and an uncle were probably killed in Sobibor—a death camp in the then-district of Lublin where Amon Goeth was posted temporarily before he came to Krakow.

Anat's father was a German Jew from Hanover; he escaped to Israel in 1935. His relatives who stayed behind in Germany were all killed.

After the war, Anat's father returned to Germany only once. When he came back to Israel, he told his children, "They are still the same, they haven't changed."

Anat's father hated the Germans, and he hated God for allowing it all to happen. Anat grew up with a bitter, old man for a father. But shortly before his death, he would suddenly only watch German TV and only listen to German radio stations.

Jennifer and Anat are sitting side by side on the porch of Anat's house in Kibbutz Eilot. Anat has made fresh mint tea and put dates on the table. She is barefoot, as are most people here; her blonde, shoulder-length hair is disheveled, and she is wearing a baggy T-shirt.

Children are running across the well-tended lawns. Nowadays, young families choose to live on a kibbutz because they want their children to grow up in a safe environment, close to nature and alongside other children of the same age. The communal nurseries are still here, but the children live at home with their parents. Anat says that she would not have

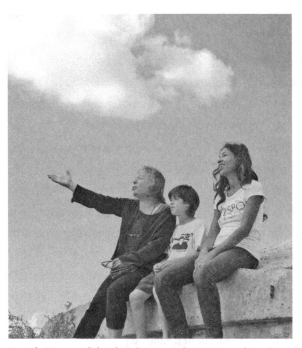

Jennifer Teege with her friend Anat and Anat's second son, Stav, in Kibbutz Eilot in 2011

joined Alon on the kibbutz if their children would have had to grow up in a children's house, as her husband did.

Today, Kibbutz Eilot is evocative of a modern townhouse complex anywhere: Children are laughing and cats are meowing; everyone knows everyone. But it has retained its strong communal spirit: There are no hedges or fences between the individual homes, and everyone pays their income into the communal pot. At the end of the day, there's not much left for the individual.

Jennifer Teege took the desert road to come here, past Bedouin settlements and signs warning of camels in the road. The longer she drove through the Negev desert, the more relaxed she seemed to become.

It has been a long journey to get to this point. She has put Krakow behind her, and a small village in Bavaria.

Jennifer and Anat are holding hands; Jennifer is stroking Anat's hand. Anat has put on Jennifer's enormous sunglasses—a fashionable model that doesn't seem quite right for her. "I'll be the talk of the kibbutz in these," Anat says and laughs.

Anat's elder son, Kai, is seventeen now—nearly the same age Anat and Jennifer were when they first met. For the last two years, Kai's history lessons have been mainly about the Holocaust. Anat says that her son is now filled with rage against the Germans.

Soon, Kai will go on a school trip to visit various concentration camps in Poland—standard practice for Israeli teenagers. Anat would like Jennifer to go with them, would like a German with her particular history to be with Kai's class when they visit Płaszów.

■ ■ ■

I HAVE TO THINK ABOUT WHETHER I want to accompany Kai and his classmates on their trip. I'd like to look forward now, not back.

We walk through the kibbutz. Anat shows me the new guesthouses. The next time I come, I want to bring my husband and my sons. I've always wanted to visit Israel as a family—but not until my children are old enough to understand this complicated country.

I hug her as we say good-bye: "Anati, my dear friend."

CHAPTER 6

FLOWERS IN KRAKOW

Everybody wants to know who they are.

—JENNIFER TEEGE'S FORMER THERAPIST AT THE UNIVERSITY
MEDICAL CENTER HAMBURG–EPPENDORF

W HAT IS FAMILY? Is it something we inherit, or something we build?

It's been exactly four years since I discovered the book about my mother, three years since I visited Krakow for the first time. When I first traveled to Poland, I had hit rock bottom. Reading the book about my mother had reopened old wounds: the hurt from my childhood, the feeling of not knowing who I am, and the sadness that had overshadowed my whole life.

Everybody wants to know where they come from, who their parents and grandparents are. Everybody wants to be able to tell their complete story, with a beginning and an end. Everybody asks: *What is unique about me?*

The book was the key to everything, the key to my life. It revealed my family secret, but the truth that lay before me was terrifying.

I went to Krakow to get closer to the overwhelming figure of Amon Goeth, to understand why he destroyed my family.

During my last visit, three years ago, I didn't have the courage to admit my identity to a Jewish tourist I happened to meet. I couldn't even tell my friends in Israel who I really was.

Those days are behind me now. I have returned to Krakow to meet my friend Anat and her son Kai. Anat has come with the class to Poland, along with a few other parents and the children's teachers.

Tomorrow, I will stand in front of Kai's class and tell them my story. How will the children react?

At first, I wasn't at all sure whether I really wanted to join them. I didn't speak to Anat about my concerns; my doubts had nothing to do with her. It was just that I had resolved not to talk about the Nazi era all the time. Not because I think it's the wrong thing to do—I think it's good that the descendants of Nazi criminals urge people to question how they are dealing with the past. But I don't want my life to revolve around just the subject of Nazism. There is an unending number of issues that are worthy of support, and I am not an expert on the Holocaust.

I decided to fulfill Anat's request anyway. After all, I wouldn't be addressing any class; it is her son Kai's class, and I'll have Anat by my side.

And I thought that it might be interesting for them to meet me. I didn't consider the impact the meeting might have on me. I had no expectations whatsoever and just wanted to take things as they came.

When I arrive at Krakow airport, I am exhausted. I haven't had time to properly prepare for my meeting with the Israeli students. I had planned on reviewing some vocab so that I could give my introduction tomorrow in Hebrew. That is out of the question now.

I have just come from the deathbed of my adoptive father. He died a few hours ago in the St. John of God Hospital in Munich. The cancer started in his prostate, but by the end it had spread all over his body.

I hail a taxicab and head toward the city. It is getting dark. In my head, I am still going over the last few days at the hospital, still sitting by Gerhard's bedside. In the past two weeks I have come to realize what it means to die. Before then, death was only an abstract concept for me.

Never before had I been with someone during the last days and weeks of their life.

It only takes a few days for a person to take their leave of this world. The body deteriorates gradually, step by step. There are so many little markers on the way to death. It is a process, and by the end every last thing has been taken from us.

When a close relative dies, we think about our own lives, too. Our own mortality, which we prefer to ignore, is suddenly very real.

When Gerhard was admitted to the hospital, he was still able to feed himself and to briefly lift himself up from the wheelchair. At first he could still drink independently, then only using a straw, and in the end not even that. He was put on a drip and a ventilator. He didn't want any life-extending procedures.

In the beginning, I would get ice cream for him; asking him which flavor he would like. "Strawberry," he would reply, or "mango" or "lemon." He could hardly eat, but the ice cream was his little pleasure.

On the day before he died, he could hardly talk anymore. When I asked him what flavor ice cream he wanted, he couldn't decide. I got some lemon ice cream for him and carefully fed him small spoonfuls. His mouth was so dry, his face so gaunt—he looked like death itself.

Gerhard kept wanting to sit up in bed because it was easier to for him breathe in that position. But the doctors said that we were not allowed to sit him up: The risk of his suffering a collapse was too great. And so he would lie there, with his pleading eyes, begging us to sit him up. Seated opposite him, I felt so helpless. For him, sitting up would have meant that last bit of independence. I would have loved to do him that small favor, but even that was not allowed. At some point he gave up and lay still, with his eyes closed.

At the hospital, all the people who were close to Gerhard came together. Someone was always with him: Inge kept watch at night; during the day, my brothers, friends, and relatives would join her, as well as my husband, our sons, and I.

The only thing that was real was Gerhard's dying; everything else seemed far away. Just like the terminally ill patient who was slipping into timelessness, into the twilight of the in-between world, we, his companions, also lost all sense of day and night.

Gerhard had enough time to say good-bye to his friends and family, properly, consciously. A blessing.

The big question was whether or not Gerhard would make it to his seventieth birthday. That had been his last wish—to celebrate his birthday surrounded by his family.

On the morning of his birthday, we all gathered around his hospital bed. My brother Manuel's daughter had baked a cake.

Gerhard opened his eyes only briefly. He was barely conscious, but he sensed that we had all come. I think he still enjoyed his birthday; it was a nice way to say good-bye. We spent the whole day taking turns by his bedside. Quietly I was hoping that he would die soon. I knew that's what he wanted, too.

Shortly after I left the hospital, Gerhard passed away.

I was onboard a plane three hours later.

Three years ago, I hadn't let a recent miscarriage prevent me from traveling to Krakow. And now it hadn't occurred to me to cancel on Anat.

My journey to Poland had been a long time in planning. I had booked my flight to Krakow weeks ago. It is part of my nature to honor my commitments.

The taxicab stops in front of a large hotel in the Podgorze area of Krakow, the former Jewish ghetto. Tomorrow, I will meet Anat and Kai, Kai's class, and his teachers. It has been nearly a year since I last saw Anat and Kai in Israel. I am looking forward to seeing them again.

■　■　■

Płaszów is the penultimate stop for the Israeli students on their tour of Poland.

In the last few days, they have visited the former Warsaw ghetto and the former extermination camp Treblinka, northeast of Warsaw. They have cleared Jewish graves of dirt and leaves and have talked at length with Auschwitz survivor Zvi Moldovan, an old, friendly Israeli who has been accompanying students on school trips to Poland for years.

At the defunct train station in Lodz, the students boarded an old cattle car which was used to transport Jews and Romany from the Lodz ghetto to the concentration camps. Inside the cattle car, it was dark and crowded. The teens tried to relate to how the Jews locked in this car must have felt. One of the Israeli girls began to tremble violently.

The students visited the Chelmno concentration camp, and later Lublin and the Majdanek camp.

They visited the former Tarnow ghetto and the Belzec camp.

The class shared a joint diary, in which every student was invited to write. One student wrote: "Numerous members of my family were murdered there. When I looked at the gas chambers, the barracks, and the crematoria, it seemed as if they had only been built yesterday. But I went there in an air-conditioned bus; my grandfather in a hot and crowded cattle car without food or water. My journey took a couple of hours; Grandfather's took three days and three nights. I was there with many of my friends; Grandfather was all alone. I left after a few hours; Grandfather left in the summer of 1944. In Poland, I saw my grandfather's memories with my own eyes. He survived and told me all about his experiences. I will always remember him."

Another student commented: "My grandmother never really escaped the camp. She was always restless and lived in constant fear of losing control over her life again. She planned and prepared things a long time in advance, forever filling her fridge and her larder. I never saw her sitting still."

Halfway through the trip, the teachers gave the students letters that their parents had written in advance. The mothers and fathers had written comforting words, asking their children not to let the terrifying sights send them into despair. Many students started crying when they read their parents' letters.

The last entry in the class diary reads: "Every day here feels like a week. I miss my parents and home so much."

At Sobibor, the students walked through the woods where the escaped prisoners once went into hiding after the unsuccessful uprising in the camp.

They went to the village of Markova in southeastern Poland, where a Polish peasant and his family once hid two Jewish families on their farm. The Germans eventually discovered the Jews and shot them dead, along with their Polish hosts: the farmers and their six young children.

One student wrote in the diary: "I no longer want to join the army. Yes, I have to defend my country, but isn't that what every soldier thinks? Isn't that what the Germans thought, too?"

Another student wrote: "How can it be that the men got up in the morning, drank their coffee, kissed their wives and children good-bye, and then went to work—work that meant degrading and killing people?"

When the students arrive in Krakow, they are exhausted. They have seen little of the country itself. To them, Poland is first and foremost a collection of killing sites.

Remembrance is one of the key values in Judaism. *Zachor*—"Remember!"—it says in the Torah. How the Holocaust and its victims are remembered, however, has changed in the years since the state of Israel was founded in 1948.

By 1949, 350,000 Shoah survivors had come to Israel. They were received with reservation. In the words of Israeli historian Moshe Zimmermann, they were regarded as "lambs that had allowed themselves to be led to the slaughter." The newly established state of Israel needed heroes and warriors, not victims.

The trauma experienced by the survivors became a taboo: In Israel, their suffering was barely mentioned in public.

The Israeli newspaper *Haaretz* once even declared: "Let's face it: The few Jews we have left in Europe are not necessarily the crème de la crème of our people." Historian Tom Segev discovered that "the Jews in Palestine were fixated on the idea that only the worst elements of society could have survived the camps, in other words, those who would steal the bread of their fellow inmates, etc. The good ones, they thought, had all been killed."

The trial of Adolf Eichmann in Israel in 1961 provided a turning point. Eichmann was responsible for the mass deportation of the European Jews to ghettos and concentration camps. The Israeli chief prosecutor not only put forward files and papers, but also, most notably, summoned many eyewitnesses who spoke openly of their pain and suffering for the first time. According to Tom Segev, the trial "released a whole generation of survivors" and served as "some kind of national group therapy."

Remembering the Shoah became a national purpose, a central, identity-establishing element of the state of Israel, which has lost none of its importance today. Just like elementary and high school teachers, caregivers in Israeli preschools and kindergartens are encouraged to educate children age-appropriately on the Shoah.

The Israeli Ministry of Education also developed a program around school trips to Poland. Since 1988, tens of thousands of children have taken part.

Great care is taken to prepare the teenagers for these journeys, which are not compulsory. When Anat and the other parents discussed whether it is right to expose the children to these horrors, some decided against the trip.

Anat wasn't worried that her son Kai would return from Poland frightened and disturbed. "My worry was rather that he would end up hating the Germans and seeing himself only as a victim of persecution."

On their bus to Krakow, the students rewatched the film *Schindler's List*. The image of Ralph Fiennes as the cruel killer Amon Goeth will still be fresh in their minds when they hear Jennifer Teege's story in Płaszów.

That's why it was so important to Anat that her friend come to Płaszów: "It's too easy to hate Amon Goeth. If the Germans and their allies can turn into murderers, then we, too, can become murderers. If the Germans could turn a blind eye, it can happen to us. I hope that my sons will always remember that. I hope that they will always see the Palestinians as human beings, not as enemies."

Upon their arrival in Krakow, the Israeli teenagers are escorted by three security guards: a bodyguard who has traveled with them from Israel, and two local policemen. They are even more watchful than usual: Four days ago, in Bulgaria, a suicide bomber attacked a passenger bus carrying Israeli tourists; six people died. The Lebanese Hezbollah militia is suspected to have been behind the attack.

The security guards check the bus every time before the children get on board; they inspect every accommodation in advance. The hotel meets all the security requirements: Each level can only be accessed through key-card-operated doors. The rooms for the Israelis are all on the same floor.

Once the teenagers have moved their bags into their rooms, they meet in the hotel lobby, where they rest for a while on modern, pastel sofas between artificial palm trees.

The boys and girls are whispering and giggling; they are planning secret meetings in their rooms. Just like on any ordinary school trip. The teenagers who live on kibbutzim are easily spotted: They walk around the stylish hotel lobby with its dark floor tiles in bare feet. A few men in suits look at them, irritated.

Kai, too, is walking around barefoot. He is the only student in the group who knows that Jennifer Teege will join them in Płaszów. Other than him, only the teachers and the accompanying parents have been told.

■　■　■

NIGHT HAS FALLEN BY THE TIME I enter the hotel in Krakow.

The following day, I meet the Israelis in town. Anat gives me a long hug.

The students have already been to the former ghetto in Podgorze and the Jewish quarter of Kazimierz with its synagogues. Now, for the first time on their trip, they have some free time in the center of Krakow. They want to shop in the Rynek, the historical market square, for souvenirs and gifts for those at home. The trip to the Płaszów memorial is planned for the afternoon.

While the students are walking around by themselves, Anat and I find a secluded café to talk. I tell her about Gerhard, his death. She is grateful that I was still able to come. I tell her that I'll have to return to Munich the next day to prepare for Gerhard's funeral with Inge and my brothers. I want to say good-bye to Gerhard, want to see him in the mortuary chapel before his body is cremated.

Anat shares my pain. She knew Gerhard; she met him when he came to see me in Israel and at my wedding. Anat says that she took to my adoptive father, but that she found the discussions he wanted to have with her, about Hitler and the Third Reich, exhausting.

Even on his deathbed, Gerhard was still thinking about the Holocaust. He wanted to talk to me about Adolf Eichmann; he had read a few books about his trial.

For many years, Gerhard looked into everything related to the Nazis. He did research, read historical sources, compared the numbers of victims. He probed deeper wherever he thought he'd discovered inaccuracies or contradictions.

He became deeply absorbed in the subject. Within the family it played only a minor role, but he had heated discussions with his friends about it—so much so that some of those friendships were destroyed.

Before he died, I suggested to him that he make up with some of those friends. But he didn't want to apologize. My brothers and I couldn't understand why he was so unrelenting, right up to the end.

On his sickbed, he also spoke about Amon Goeth. He quoted Dostoyevsky and asked if man was evil. We discussed the theses put forward by Alexander and Margarete Mitscherlich, who claimed that most Germans were unable to feel guilt or shame after the war. Again, I was unsure what Gerhard was driving at.

I don't think that he could quite put his finger on what exactly was bothering him. He hid behind quotations and theories. But ultimately, it boiled down to his parents. It was all about his own childhood, his mother and his father.

They weren't party members, but were sympathizers and followers. They liked the discipline and the Hitler Youth, and they believed in the secure future that Hitler promised. Opa Bochum regarded the Nazis' success as a blessing for Germany.

In his dying days, Gerhard spoke for the first time at length about his parents: Oma and Opa Bochum.

■   ■   ■

Matthias Sieber, the elder of Jennifer Teege's adoptive brothers, believes that, in many discussions, his father was subconsciously trying to defend his parents. Gerhard Sieber was plagued by the question of whether the German people knew about the extermination camps during World War II: "My father knew that the deportations and the disappearance of so many people could not have gone unnoticed. He was asking himself whether his parents had been aware of anything."

Gerhard's parents were keen on Hitler's ideas, and enamored of the man himself: "In the nineteen-fifties, my grandfather once said to my father that Hitler wasn't dead at all and was sure to come back soon. Later, my father regretted not asking his father what he meant by that."

Gerhard Sieber's father died young. Gerhard later tried to talk to his mother about the Nazi years. She claimed not to have known anything about the killing of the Jews.

She once told Matthias that one of the reasons behind the anti-Semitism was the fact that the Jews had owned all the department stores before the war.

Matthias thinks: "My father carried around this unresolved conflict with his parents. He grappled with the Holocaust without realizing that what he really wanted to understand was his parents."

■ ■ ■

THE TEACHERS ARE CALLING THE CHILDREN to get ready to leave. We board the bus and drive to the site of the former Płaszów concentration camp.

I am sitting next to one of Kai's classmates. I don't know her; she doesn't say anything. A few others are eyeing me with curiosity. They don't yet know who I am; I am still traveling incognito. Anat and the teachers thought it would best to wait until we got to the memorial before telling them who I am. I lean back and close my eyes; I can rest now before the official part begins.

I don't have any expectations for the day. I only know what I don't want to do, and that's to impart knowledge. That's a job for schoolteachers and university professors. Facts are important; we need them to gain a deeper understanding of things. But if nothing else follows upon the facts, if they are not connected to anything real, nor reflected upon, then they are of little value. They are forgotten as soon as they are heard.

The Israeli students have learned much about the victims on this school trip, and also something about those on other side, the perpetrators. They must be asking themselves: How could it have happened that some people killed millions of other people?

I want to tell the story from a different perspective. I want to tell them what it is like to be the granddaughter of a concentration camp commandant. And I want to tell them about my relationship with Anat.

Neither Anat nor I knew about my family history when we met by chance. She is a descendant of the generation of victims, I am a descendant of the generation of perpetrators. Nevertheless, our relationship is not symbolic; it is a true friendship that has lasted to this day.

The bus stops by the side of the highway that runs along the boundary of the old camp, and we get off. Once again, I walk up the hill toward the memorial.

The last time I came here, I didn't know what to do with the new information about my family. But I felt there had to be something useful about knowing the horrific truth. I had lived half a life unaware of my origins, but now I had the truth at last. The knowledge shocked me, but it also released me.

Family secrets are corrosive. How often did I despair, feeling like I'd arrived at yet another locked door?

Discovering my family's secret pulled the rug out from under my depression. I felt better after my first trip to Krakow. Today, my sadness is gone.

The first time I came to Krakow, I was still hoping to see my mother again and to build a new relationship with her. It didn't happen. I found her and lost her again.

But I still have my adoptive family.

For a long time, I struggled with my adoptive parents. More than anything, I noticed our differences—everything that separated us. But as Gerhard was dying, I realized how much we have in common. We have spent so many years together and have shared so many experiences. I belong to this family now.

During Gerhard's illness, we were there for each other. It was a wonderful feeling, to be part of a family. When we were planning Gerhard's seventieth birthday at the hospital, Matthias and I went to the house in Waldtrudering and retrieved Oma Bochum's old coffee set and the matching tablecloth from the basement. It has a flower motif, which we all—my adoptive father, his sister and foster siblings, and also my brothers and I—have known since our childhood days.

When we laid the table at the hospital, all the generations present remembered that coffee set. To any outsider, it would have been just some old-fashioned crockery and a patterned tablecloth.

We arrive at the memorial. The students sit down on the steps; the teachers, Anat, and I remain standing before them. One of the teachers says a few introductory words about the Płaszów camp and about its commandant, Amon Goeth.

Next, Anat begins to speak. She describes how I showed up one day at her shared apartment in Tel Aviv that day over twenty years ago, how our friendship has grown and endured to this day. I am touched by her speech.

Anat passes the microphone on to me. I greet the students with "shalom" and go on to describe how I grew up, how I only recently came to discover my family secret. I explain why I stopped writing to Anat and how glad I am to be here with her today. I don't find it hard to tell my story. I tell the students that I will be happy to answer any questions they might have. I want a dialog with them. I don't want to give a lecture; I want to learn something new myself.

■　■　■

At first, some of the students are inattentive as they stand in front of the Płaszów memorial. There is nothing to see but the monument and the green grass. A few of them are already thinking about the next item on the agenda: There will be folk music tonight, something cheerful at last—Polish dancers in traditional costumes, the women wearing flowers in their hair, the men with pointed hats on their heads. The Israeli teenagers will clap and dance, too. The following morning they will be heading to Auschwitz, a sad ending to their trip. Some are afraid of going to Auschwitz.

When Jennifer Goeth starts to explain that she is the granddaughter of Amon Goeth, the students perk up. Some nudge the person next to them: *Who is she? Amon Goeth, how? But she's got dark skin, and she lived in Israel. How can that be?* Many students look shocked, some begin to cry and wipe away their tears with their sleeves. One boy quickly puts on his sunglasses.

The children have many questions. "Was your grandmother a Nazi, too? How did she live in the camp?" "Are you in contact with neo-Nazis?" "How do you cope with it all?" The students' biology teacher wants to know: "Are you afraid of your genes?"

A petite girl with long, dark curls remarks that she knows a lot about the second- and third-generation descendants of the victims, but nothing about their persecutors' descendants: "When Jennifer told us her story, I understood that she and her family are also scarred, in their own way. That she also suffered a trauma." Before she went to Poland, the girl's parents had told her: "Even though everything will be very sad, retain your belief in the good in mankind, in everyone." It's these words that come to her mind now.

Another girl says that she felt an obligation to be touched, to be moved on this trip, which sometimes was a burden: What if she didn't feel anything? But the girl acknowledges: "Jennifer's story, that moved me."

For each commemorative site they are visiting, a group of students has prepared a little ceremony: writing speeches, picking songs, and choosing the color of the flowers. In Płaszów, the ritual is about to begin: One of the young Israelis puts on his yarmulke and gets out his guitar.

Dusk is falling. Joggers are running past; people are walking their dogs. The three security guards accompanying the class have spread out over the area of the former Płaszów camp, climbing the small hills in order to get a clear overview. They coordinate via cell phones while the students prepare for the ceremony, sheets of paper with their speeches at the ready.

■ ■ ■

IT WAS GOOD TO SPEAK in front of the students. They listened spellbound; no one was distracted. I looked into their faces and saw their eyes widen, saw them connecting the past to the present. Afterward, they bombarded me with questions; they wanted to know how I am doing now.

Now they walk up to the memorial; the ceremony begins. Some students read their own compositions in Hebrew; others read testimonies from Płaszów survivors. Then one of the girls sings a

The Israeli students at the Płaszów memorial, in 2012

song, accompanied by one of the boys on guitar. I stand on the edge with Kai and Anat, listening.

Suddenly, one of the Israeli girls by the memorial waves me over: She invites me to take part in their ceremony commemorating the Płaszów victims. I walk to the front; the students take me into their midst. The girl who was going to lay down the flowers gives me a hug. She hands me the bunch of red roses and asks me to lay them down for the class.

I am surprised. At first I hesitate and whisper "no." I am touched by the students' gesture, but I am not sure if it is right for me to perform the ritual. If I am the right person to do it.

The first time I came to Krakow, I brought my own flowers with me and laid them down in private. This time, it is better. This time, I am not alone.

I pause for a second. Then I step forward. I stop in front of the memorial and slowly place the flowers on the stone. And then we sing "Hatikvah," the Israeli national anthem.

Hatikvah means "hope."

BOOKS, FILMS AND ONLINE

About Amon Goeth, Ruth Irene Goeth, and their daughter Monika

BOOKS:

Awtuszewka-Ettrich, Angelina. "Płaszów – Stammlager," in *Der Ort des Terrors: Geschichte der nationalsozialistischen Konzentrationslager,* Bd. 8 [The place of terror: History of the Nazi concentration camps, Vol. 8]. Edited by Wolfgang Benz and Barbara Distel, 235–87. Munich: Verlag C. H. Beck, 2008.

Crowe, David. M. *Oskar Schindler: The Untold Account of His Life, Wartime Activities, and the True Story Behind the List.* Berkeley: Westview Press, 2004.

Keneally, Thomas. *Schindler's List.* New York: Simon & Schuster, 1994. Originally published as *Schindler's Ark* (London: Hodder & Stoughton, 1982).

Kessler, Matthias. *"Ich muß doch meinen Vater lieben, oder?" Die Lebensgeschichte von Monika Göth, Tochter des KZ-Kommandanten aus "Schindlers Liste"* [I have to love my father, don't I? The life story of Monika Goeth, daughter of the concentration camp commandant from *Schindler's List*]. Frankfurt: Eichborn Verlag, 2002.

Pemper, Mietek. *The Road to Rescue: The Untold Story of Schindler's List.* Translated by David Dollenmayer. New York: Other Press, 2011. Originally published in German as *Der rettende Weg: Schindlers Liste. Die wahre Geschichte.* (Hamburg: Hoffmann und Campe Verlag, 2005).

Sachslehner, Johannes. *Der Tod ist ein Meister aus Wien: Leben und Taten des Amon Leopold Göth* [Death is a master from Vienna: The life and deeds of Amon Leopold Goeth]. Vienna: Styria Premium, 2008.

Segev, Tom. *Soldiers of Evil: The Commandants of the Nazi Concentration Camps*. Translated by Haim Watzman. New York: McGraw-Hill, 1988. Originally published in Hebrew as *Hayale ha-resha* (Jerusalem: Domino Press, 1987).

FILMS:

Blair, Jon. *Schindler: The Real Story*. HBO Home Video, 2001. Originally *Schindler: Die Dokumentation* [Schindler: The documentary]. UK, 1983. PolyGram-Video 1993.

Kessler, Matthias. *Amons Tochter* [Amon's daughter]. Germany, 2003.

Moll, James. *Inheritance*. Allentown Productions, 2006. Film: pbs.org/pov/inheritance/; Panel discussion, 2008: pbs.org/pov/inheritance/video_panel.php.

Spielberg, Steven. *Schindler's List*. Universal, 1993.

Ze'evi, Chanoch. *Hitler's Children*. Israel, 2011. hitlerschildren.com.

WEB:

A series of interviews by Mietek Pemper with Monika Hertwig: mietek-pemper.de/wiki/Interview_mit_Monika_Hertwig.

Selected reports of Płaszów survivors

Frister, Roman. *The Cap: The Price of a Life*. Translated by Hillel Halkin. New York: Grove Press, 1999. Originally published in Hebrew as *Deyokan 'atsmi 'im tsaleket* (Tel Aviv: Devir, 1993).

Müller-Madej, Stella. *A Girl from Schindler's List*. Translated by William R. Brand. London: Polish Cultural Foundation, 1997. Originally published in German as *Das Mädchen von der Schindler-Liste* (Augsburg: Olive Tree Publishing, 1994).

About other descendants of perpetrators

BOOKS:

Brunner, Claudia, and Uwe von Seltmann. *Schweigen die Täter, reden die Enkel* [When the perpetrators keep silent, their grandchildren will talk]. Frankfurt: Fischer Verlag, 2006.

Frank, Niklas. *In the Shadow of the Reich*. Translated by Arthur S. Wensinger. New York: Knopf, 1991. Originally published in German as *Der Vater: Eine Abrechnung* (Munich: Verlag C. Bertelsmann, 1987).

Frank, Niklas. *Meine deutsche Mutter* [My German mother]. Munich: Verlag C. Bertelsmann, 2005.

Himmler, Katrin. *The Himmler Brothers: A German Family History*. Translated by Michael Mitchell. London: Macmillan, 2007. Originally published in German as *Die Brüder Himmler: Eine deutsche Familiengeschichte* (Frankfurt: S. Fischer Verlag, 2005).

Lebert, Norbert, and Stephan Lebert. *My Father's Keeper*. Translated by Julian Evans. Boston: Little, Brown, 2001. Originally published in German as *Denn Du trägst meinen Namen: Das schwere Erbe der prominenten Nazi-Kinder* (Munich: Karl Blessing Verlag, 2000).

Nissen, Margret. *Sind Sie die Tochter Speer?* [Are you Speer's daughter?]. Munich: Deutsche Verlags-Anstalt, 2004.

Saur, Karl-Otto, and Michael Saur. *Er stand in Hitlers Testament: Ein deutsches Familienerbe* [He was named in Hitler's will: A German family legacy]. Berlin: Econ Verlag, 2007.

Senfft, Alexandra. *Schweigen tut weh: Eine deutsche Familiengeschichte* [Silence hurts: A German family history]. Berlin: Claassen Verlag, 2007.

Schirach, Richard von. *Der Schatten meines Vaters* [My father's shadow]. Munich: Carl Hanser Verlag, 2005.

Timm, Uwe. *In My Brother's Shadow*. Translated by Anthea Bell. London: Bloomsbury, 2005. Originally published in German as *Am Beispiel meines Bruders* (Cologne: Verlag Kiepenheuer & Witsch, 2003).

FILM:

Ludin, Malte. *2 or 3 Things I Know About Him*. National Center for Jewish Film, 2007. Originally *2 oder 3 Dinge, die ich von ihm weiß* (Germany, 2005), absolut Medien, 2oder3dinge.de.

About the psychology of perpetrators and followers, of second and third generations of descendants of Nazi criminals, plus general information about trauma therapy

Bar-On, Dan. *Legacy of Silence: Encounters with Children of the Third Reich*. Cambridge: Harvard University Press, 1989.

Kellner, Friedrich. *Vernebelt, verdunkelt sind alle Hirne: Tagebücher 1939–1945* [They see no evil, hear no evil: Diaries 1939–1945]. Edited by Sascha Feuchert, Robert Kellner, Erwin Leibfried, Jörg Riecke, and Markus Roth. Göttingen: Wallstein Verlag, 2011.

Kogan, Ilany. *Der stumme Schrei der Kinder: Die zweite Generation der Holocaust-Opfer* [The silent scream of the children: The second generation of Holocaust victims]. Frankfurt: S. Fischer Verlag, 1998.

Mitscherlich, Alexander and Margarete Mitscherlich. *The Inability to Mourn: Principles of Collective Behavior*. Translated by Beverley R. Placzek. New York: Grove Press, 1975. Originally published in German as *Die Unfähigkeit zu trauern: Grundlagen kollektiven Verhaltens* (Munich: Piper Verlag, 1967).

Ruppert, Franz. *Trauma, Bonding & Family Constellations: Understanding and Healing Injuries of the Soul*. West Sussex: Green Balloon Publishing, 2008. Originally published in German as *Trauma, Bindung und Familienstellen: Seelische Verletzungen verstehen und heilen*. (Stuttgart: Klett-Cotta Verlag, 2007).

Welzer, Harald, Sabine Moller and Karoline Tschuggnall. *"Opa war kein Nazi": Nationalsozialismus und Holocaust im Familiengedächtnis* [Grandpa wasn't a Nazi: National Socialism and the Holocaust in family memory]. Frankfurt: S. Fischer Verlag, 2002.

Welzer, Harald. *Täter. Wie aus ganz normalen Menschen Massenmörder werden* [Perpetrators. How ordinary people become mass murderers]. Frankfurt: S. Fischer Verlag, 2005.

Westerhagen, Dörte von. *Die Kinder der Täter: Das Dritte Reich und die Generation danach* [The children of the perpetrators: The Third Reich and the next generation]. Munich: Kösel Verlag, 1987.

Yalom, Irvin D. *Staring at the Sun: Overcoming the Terror of Death*. San Francisco: John Wiley & Sons, 2008. Published in Germany as *Der Panama-Hut oder Was einen guten Therapeuten ausmacht* (Munich: Goldmann Verlag, 2002).

Other

Nattiv, Guy. *Mabul (The Flood)*. Scripted by Noa Berman-Herzberg and Guy Nattiv. Israel: K5 International Producers, 2011.

Special Note

If you are interested in looking into your own family history of the Nazi era, you can find exceptional guidance here (in German): https://chrismon.evangelisch.de/comment/21672.

ABOUT THE AUTHORS

JENNIFER TEEGE has worked in advertising since 1999. She lived for four years in Israel, where she became fluent in Hebrew. She holds a degree from Tel Aviv University in Middle Eastern and African studies. Teege lives in Germany with her husband and two sons. This is her first book. For more information about Jennifer Teege, please visit jennifer-teege.com.

NIKOLA SELLMAIR graduated from Ludwig-Maximilians-University Munich and has worked in Hong Kong, Washington, D.C., Israel, and Palestine. She has been a reporter in Hamburg at Germany's *Stern* magazine since 2000. Her work has received many awards, including the German-Polish Journalist Award, for the first-ever article about Jennifer Teege's singular story.

■　■　■

ABOUT THE TRANSLATOR

Born in Germany, CAROLIN SOMMER studied applied languages at universities in Germany, France, and the UK before settling in the UK in 1997. After working in bilingual roles for multinational companies for several years, she took a career break to look after her three sons. Translations have been her career focus since 2011.

OKANAGAN REGIONAL LIBRARY
3 3132 03712 4767